THAT TAKES THE

Cake

Book of Comfort
Book of Friendship
Book of Good Advice
Book of the Year
How Did It Begin?
How Did Sex Begin?
Mistakes, Misnomers and Misconceptions
Strange Customs
Thank God I'm an Atheist
There's a Reason for Everything

THAT TAKES THE
Cake

R. BRASCH

Angus&Robertson
An imprint of HarperCollins*Publishers*

An Angus & Robertson Publication

Angus & Robertson, an imprint of
HarperCollins Publishers,
25 Ryde Road, Pymble, Sydney NSW 2073, Australia.
31 View Road, Glenfield, Auckland 10, New Zealand.

First published in Australia in 1994.

National Library of Australia
Cataloguing-in-Publication data:
    Brasch, R. (Rudolph), 1912–
    That takes the cake.
    Includes index.
    ISBN 0 207 18563 8.
    1. English language—Terms and phrases. 2. Figures of speech. 3. English
    language—Etymology. I. Title.

422

Cover illustration by Steven Bray.
Printed by Griffin Paperbacks, Adelaide.

9 8 7 6 5 4 3 2 1
98 97 96 95 94

CONTENTS

PREFACE

It is my sincere hope that this book will become a permanent part of your library of knowledge, both as a reference book and for enjoyable reading. *That Takes the Cake* brings together the past and the present and gives food for thought on the working of our minds and the evolution of society. To study the beginnings of words, idioms and traditions not only helps us to understand our origins but also helps us to understand ourselves.

The wealth of information contained in the origins of what we say and do is remarkable. Everyday phrases and traditions that we take for granted have an intriguing history, and their origins are full of interest. Customs, often practised thoughtlessly, have a profound meaning and, at times, an extraordinary background in etymology, incident, fact or folklore. Even superstitions, if traced to their sources, once had a significant motivation. This book explains over 350 such origins. It opens windows on aspects of culture and history often unseen or unexpected, and clarifies many expressions and traditions that bewilder us.

Covering a wide range of topics, the exploration of beginnings extends from all kinds of supposed trivia to the monumental 'juggernaut', from the ominous '666, the number of the Beast' to 'zilch', from a 'one-night stand' to the 'upper crust'. The book investigates the reason why, paradoxically, a company closing down is said to be 'wound up' and why some things just 'go to the dogs'.

All the explanations reflect the colourful make-up of our culture and our rich heritage. Who put the hole in the doughnut and why is there a dot on the 'i'? What led to the description of a critical life situation as a 'Catch 22'? How did the black and white chequered flag find its place in motor racing, and why are the gondolas in Venice painted black?

To find out origins is an exciting pursuit, with many surprises and revelations. Customs apparently meaningless today, observed out of mere habit or etiquette, may be a relic of humanity's fight for survival or for a cause once cherished, and show humanity's creative gift for preserving the obsolete by transforming and adapting it to the present day's needs. Examples include the still-observed custom of newly weds not to reveal even to their best friends the destination of their honeymoon; or the American way of eating; or the modern use of teabags.

Phrases and terms of the past which have stayed with us now serve a totally different, if not contrary, purpose from that for which they were first created. The 'skeleton in the cupboard' was once exactly that, and it served a positive and essential function.

Apart from all these different topics, this book relates many an enchanting story. It gives the delightful interpretation of the kink in a Siamese cat's tail and tells why a beautiful Australian parrot became known as the Rosella.

The material is arranged alphabetically. You may read this book from cover to cover or just pick it up and select any item that takes your fancy or arouses your curiosity. There is much, I hope, that will give you something to remember, to discuss and to talk about. Fact and fiction, material researched world wide and in depth, entertaining anecdotes, and figments of the imaginations of people trying to make sense out of the weird, the unusual or incomprehensible are presented.

I am grateful to many readers and listeners for the questions they have put to me, questions that I hope I have gone some way to answering in this volume. Last, but not least, my wife, once again, deserves special mention. Without her, this book, like all my other books, would never have been written. As always, she has been my constant companion, help and inspiration.

R. *Brasch*

To the many listeners,
readers and correspondents who contributed to this book
by asking questions.

ABOVE BOARD

For anything to be 'above board' suggests complete honesty. There is no subterfuge. Nothing is concealed and therefore open to doubt or suspicion. Yet, so incongruously, the origin of the phrase is uncertain and two possible, totally unconnected explanations have been given.

All that is 'above board' may have started at sea—on board ship. Not stowed (or hidden) away in the holds under hatches, it is on deck, for all to see.

The nefarious practice of cardsharpers has equally been linked, though in a negative way, with the saying. To cheat their opponents, surreptitiously they would exchange cards under the gaming table with their accomplices. The honest player—to avoid even the slightest suspicion of foul play—would always keep his hands 'above [the] board'.

ACHILLES HEEL

When speaking of a person's Achilles heel, we refer to their only vulnerable spot. The figure of speech is based on a Greek myth which tells how Achilles' mother, to make her son's body unassailable and safe from the infliction of a mortal wound, dipped the baby into the river Styx. She did not realise then that though the waters covered his entire body, not so the one heel by which she held him. It was an omission for which he had to pay with his life!

Paris, his arch-enemy in the Trojan War, was aware of Achilles' unprotected heel. By piercing it with an arrow, he slew the principal hero of the *Iliad*.

ADDING INSULT TO INJURY

Not satisfied with having inflicted bodily harm, some people aggravate the damage they have done by further hurting their victim with wounding words. They 'add insult to injury', as the saying goes.

Unfortunately, it must have been a human failing from early on, as the descriptive phrase goes back to one of *Aesop's Fables*, quoted by Phaedrus, the first-century Roman author.

The fable tells of a fly biting a bald man on his head. Trying to kill it, he not only missed the insect but hit himself. Highly amused and happy to have escaped the blow, the fly now addressed the man. 'You intended to kill me for a mere touch,' it said. 'What will you do to yourself, now that you have added insult to injury!' The legendary fly's words are the source of the so modern-sounding phrase!

AFTERMATH

In spite of modern urbanisation, many terms of everyday life recall the rural roots of civilisation and society's original close contact with nature. Thus to call the follow-up of an event its inevitable consequence (mainly when this is of an unfortunate nature, as in the case of disaster and war) goes back to the soil and farm life.

'Math' from the Old English *meath*, originally referred to 'mowing', the harvesting of the grass, then done with a scythe or a sickle. Once this crop, which provided the best sort of hay, had been gathered, new shoots came up. They were public property and therefore welcomed by landless people. It was their chance to reap for themselves (like the biblical gleaning) the new growth. This, very much to the point, came to be known as the 'aftermowing'—the aftermath.

ALIMONY

Cynics have suggested that alimony stood for 'all his money'. Linguistically, there is no mention of money at all in the legal term. Nor is this allowance to a divorced wife regarded as 'alms', as dissatisfied parties have been led to believe. The *mony* of the word has merely grammatical significance. It is a common suffix without pecuniary meaning and occurs in such diverse conditions and occasions as matri*mony*, acri*mony* and cere*mony*. The decisive part of alimony is contained in *ali*, its first half. From the Latin for 'nourishment' and 'sustenance', it is also found in the *ali*mentary canal. Alimony thus speaks of ensuring that the divorced spouse will not go hungry.

ARMAGEDDON

Armageddon has become a figure of speech for a cataclysmic clash between opposing powers, representing irreconcilable ideologies and interests. The resulting most frightful devastation and slaughter would lead to the end of the world.

Actually, the term now synonymous with the horrendous prophecy is the corrupt rendering of the name of a geographical site. Situated in the north of the Holy Land, 35 kilometres (22 miles) southeast of Haifa, it was known in the Hebrew tongue as *Har Megiddo* (the mountain of Megiddo) or *Ir Megiddo* (the city of Megiddo). Transposed into Greek, the name was disfigured into Armageddon and first appears as such in the New Testament.

Strategically positioned on the crossroads between east and west, 'the mountain of Megiddo' repeatedly—from the most ancient days to modern times—has been the scene of decisive battles, sometimes so momentous that they changed the course of history.

It was at Megiddo—in 609 BC—that Josiah, a most revered king of Judah, fell in battle. As an ally of the Babylonians, he had tried to stop their Egyptian enemy joining the Syrian forces. In the ensuing action, he was slain.

His loss was regarded as so disastrous for the nation that people came to identify the name of Megiddo, already linked with so many battles, bloodshed and defeats, with a shattering catastrophe.

This, no doubt, prompted Christian tradition, as recorded in the Book of Revelation (16:16–21), to make *Har Megiddo*, Armageddon in its new spelling, the site of the final great battle of the world. A confrontation between the forces of good and evil, its scope would not only be of global but of cosmic proportions:

> ...and there were thunders and lightnings; and there was a great earthquake, such as was not since men were upon the earth, so mighty an earthquake, and so great...and every island vanished, and the mountains were not found...and a great hail...fell down out of heaven upon men...

Significantly, Megiddo came to play an historic role once again in modern times. General Allenby of Britain launched his offensive against the Turks from there on 18 September 1918, resulting in their ultimate defeat. When, on 2 September 1945, General Douglas MacArthur accepted the Japanese surrender in Tokyo Bay, he remembered the ancient city's place in its eschatological context. He used it as a warning. Mankind, he said, had had its last chance to determine the future of the world by means of war. Indeed, if no other peaceful solution was found, 'Armageddon will be at our door.'

BACK TO SQUARE ONE

BALDERDASH

BALLYHOO

BARGE IN

BATTING AN EYE(LID)

BAWDY

BESIDE ONESELF

BESIDE THE MARK

BIG APPLE

BIRTHDAY CARDS

BIRTHDAY CELEBRATIONS

BISTRO

BITE THE BULLET

BITING REMARKS

BLACKBALL

BLACK BOOK OR BLACKLISTED

BLACK DAYS

BLARNEY

BLAZE A TRAIL

BLOW HOT AND COLD

BLOW ONE'S TOP

BLOW A RASPBERRY

BLUDGER

BLUE MONDAY

BOB'S YOUR UNCLE

BONKERS

BRAND NEW

BRIDESMAIDS AND GROOMSMEN

BRING DOWN THE HOUSE

BROWBEAT

BROWNED OFF

BRUMBY

BUCKLEY'S CHANCE

BUGS AND BUGGING

BUTTONHOLE

BUTTONHOLE WORN AT A WEDDING

BY AND LARGE

BY-LAWS

BACK TO SQUARE ONE

Having unsuccessfully pursued a course of action, it is often necessary to start all over again. Such reversion is remindful of some board games, like Snakes and Ladders, in which by an unlucky cast of the dice, a player is forced to return to the beginning. The player has to move the piece 'back to square [numbered] one'. The simile well-fitted the description of a like situation in life.

The phrase has also been linked with the children's game hopscotch, in which the unlucky participant has to go back to the starter square.

It has been claimed as well that the expression, if not actually created, was popularised in the early days of British radio. To help football fans follow the broadcast commentaries on matches, the BBC journal used to publish a ground plan of the field, divided into numbered 'squares'. All that was needed for the ardent listener to keep up with the game, was to look at the specific number referred to at that moment by the commentator.

The English, fond of the sport and glued to their wireless sets, soon acquired this terminology, and applied it to many other occasions, and in the case of 'back to square no. 1', retained it long after the diagram had ceased to appear.

BALDERDASH

Even 'balderdash', this gibberish talk, full of pretence but lacking any sense, has its distinctive features. The story of its past gives meaning to its meaningless words. To begin with, 'balderdash' was something real, though unsubstantial— mere froth. Its earliest use can be traced to the end of the sixteenth century. Thomas Nash, the famous English satirist, refers to it in his *Lenten Stuffe* (1599), the last work he wrote, a burlesque on red herring! He spoke of people who did not want their heads washed with 'this bubbly spume of barbers balderdash'.

A century later the foam, as it were, had liquefied, and balderdash had become a term applied to odd mixtures of drinks. These were either adulterated or concocted of such bizarre cocktails as buttermilk with beer or beer with wine! From this liquid source balderdash emerged to become a term ultimately applied to a jumble of words, incongruous, silly talk—gobbledegook.

BALLYHOO

Ballyhoo is a lot of noise—signifying nothing. It refers to the extraordinary and often ludicrous ways used to attract people's attention, exploiting their gullibility, for example, to make them buy goods they did not need, or to come to a show.

The racket ballyhoo stands for has created its own problem. It concerns not its blatant method of promotion and salesmanship, but the very origin of the expression.

Some authorities claim that the word derives from Ballyhooly, a small Irish village in the County of Cork. Even for Irish ears, it was said, its people had been particularly boisterous, noisy and full of blarney.

Others have traced the term to the United States where, from the 1890s onward, it was used in show business: by circus people, in music halls and by travelling theatrical groups. Many of them were run by Irish migrants, who still among themselves used Gaelic and spoke with a strong brogue. To attract the attention of the public and make them come to the 'show' was the specific task allotted to one member of the company. For obvious reasons, this person became known as 'the barker'. With a stentorian voice, they gave a colourful (and highly exaggerated) account of the entertainment offered, which no one could afford to miss. To be seen by all, they took their stand on a platform. This was known as a *bally*, soon to be identified with the barkers' blatant talk—all their hoo-ha. The association of the two created the *ballyhoo*.

The barkers had yet another job. During the interval, they had to 'pass round the hat', a no less important function. Making their voice heard above the din of the crowd, they announced (in their native tongue), 'Collection now!'. To American ears, the Irish words sounded very much like 'ballyhoo'.

Ballyhoo has been given an international flavour as well. It has been seen as the corrupted version of an Arab formula, acknowledging God's omnipotence and submitting to His will—B'A*llah hoo* (through God it is). It is said to have been the cry of dervishes who appeared at the World Fair in Chicago in 1893. Their call did not go unheeded. The public took it up and, as 'ballyhoo', made it part of the English language, though in a totally different sense.

Going still further afield, out to sea in fact, one etymologist has linked the term with seamen's contempt for a certain type of two-masted sailing ship they encountered in the West Indies. Noting its inadequate, odd and bad riggings, they decried it by using the Central American word for the wood from which the craft was made, *bally*. As ballyhoo it became a term of abuse others soon applied to any vessel they felt was not seaworthy, referring to it as 'ballyhoo of blazes'. Eventually, the word was used as much on land as at sea.

There is no doubt, however, that ballyhoo contains more than people want to admit. Bally once served as a swear word—among the most effective of all at the time. It was a euphemism for 'bloody'.

A favourite expression on the stage of late nineteenth-century music halls was the saying 'the whole bloody truth'.

Anticipating Shaw's famous expletive in *Pygmalion*, it would bring down the house. But to use the phrase explicitly was impossible. Actors therefore camouflaged the 'offensive' words by changing them into the respectable 'ballyhooly truth'. Finally, cut down in size, it left us with the present-day ballyhoo which, like all make-believe, is far from true.

BARGE IN

Special types of barges—flat-bottomed boats—have been used in England to ply the shallow waters of rivers and canals to transport freight. Lacking power of their own, the vessels were either propelled by poles or pulled by men or horses, walking alongside on a narrow tow-path.

The navigation of such a vessel had its hazards. Once in motion, its own impetus and lack of manoeuvrability carried it straight ahead, making it exceedingly hard to avoid obstacles in its way. By 'barging in', it caused collisions and not a few accidents. People soon adopted the phrase for other situations. They applied it to those who in conversations gave their own advice or opinion uninvited or, physically, bumped into a person or an object.

At times, the barge poles used, of necessity, were extremely long. This gave rise to yet another contribution to phraseology. It was said of people (or objects), regarded as obnoxious and repugnant, that one would not touch them with a barge pole.

BATTING AN EYE(LID)

Those showing no surprise and remaining calm in the most trying circumstances are said to 'not bat an eyelid'. They are so unconcerned and steady that not even their eyelids flicker.

The phrase comes from falconry, one of the oldest sports in the world. Hawks, employed to hunt wild quarry, prior to being let loose for their chase, were secured by a leash and made to sit on a perch, often the falconer's wrist. Struggling wildly to escape, they were said to 'bate'. Their vigorous struggle is recalled in the 'batting of an eyelid'.

BAWDY

Prostitutes have been described as members of the oldest profession. It is no wonder therefore that terms linked with their trade are numerous. Though the occupation has remained the same, the names under which they work have been updated many times.

The madam running a brothel was known in Elizabethan times as a bawdy and, accordingly, her establishment became a bawdy house. The background of the term is uncertain. Both the Old High German for 'bold' and the French for 'merry' have been quoted as its source. Some even believed that 'bawd' is all that is left of the original 'ribald', from the Old French *ribauld*. Persons were so called because of their delight in the crude and licentious.

With time, the term has mellowed and, less concerned with the sale of sex, it merely continues to be employed for references and remarks that are obscene, erotic or lewd.

BESIDE ONESELF

We speak of someone who is overwrought by some emotion or worry as being 'beside himself' or 'beside herself'. The peculiar phrase is based on the belief that every individual possesses a body and a spirit (or soul).

Experiencing a traumatic upheaval, it was imagined,

resulted in the spirit leaving the body. Having done so, it would not vanish, but remain standing next to the person—beside them—hopeful that they would regain their composure and, with it, create the right condition for the spirit to return to the body and make it ' whole again'.

BESIDE THE MARK

Anything irrelevant and not to the point is judged to be 'beside the mark'. The phrase originated in archery.

Now merely a sport, it once played an important part in English life, in the defence of the country. Citizens then practised archery not as a pastime, but as an obligatory pursuit of military importance. No village was without its highly-trained bowmen ready for any national emergency.

In their practice, bowmen competed with each other to score a maximum number of hits. A piece of cloth or leather attached to a tree served as their improvised target. Obviously, those who missed it hit the tree 'beside the mark'. Their failure left its imprint on everyday language. Anything that was irrelevant and therefore did not count—like those misses in archery—became known as 'beside the mark'.

BIG APPLE

Apples have always been a favoured fruit, and not least so in the United States. A traditional gift of pupils to their teacher, it became part of most diverse expressions. People spoke of 'upsetting the applecart', things being in 'apple-pie order' or as 'sure as God made little apples'. Sycophants were nicknamed 'apple polishers' and wiseacres 'small apples'.

Taking up a conspicuous place in the cornucopia, the horn of plenty, the apple symbolised the exquisite, tasty and enjoyable. Was it any wonder then that New York, so rich, full of promise and opportunity, became known not just as an apple, but as the 'Big Apple'—as it were, putting all other cities in the shade?

There was much more to it. In fact, this apple is not even a home-grown fruit. So typically American now, it is rooted in the Spanish tongue and can be traced not to an apple at all, but a dance!

New Orleans is the home of jazz. A vibrant and vital centre of the city is known as Manzana, the Spanish word for an apple, no doubt because it once was the site of an apple orchard. And right in its midst is the very block where jazz was born, enthusiastically played there and enjoyed. Proudly the jazz players referred to it as *Manzana Principal*, the 'main apple'.

From Louisiana the novel style of ragtime was then taken to New York, where a Harlem nightclub became the centre for jazz musicians. No doubt recalling the district in their home-town, they named it the 'Big Apple'. They were largely responsible for the spread of the name which, in mid-1953, was also adopted for the jitterbug dance. In no time, this caught on like wildfire among the people to become a veritable New York craze, soon to be identified with the city. Not slow in realising the promotional value of being described as the 'Big Apple', New York adopted it as its slogan. One of the jazz players has been credited with being the actual source of the description. He is quoted to have remarked one day that there were many apples on a tree, but to be able to perform in New York City, indeed, was the 'Big Apple'.

BIRTHDAY CARDS

Birthday cards are of comparatively recent origin. They were introduced in the latter half of the nineteenth century, soon after the first Christmas cards.

Their text was simple and to the point; it briefly wished the recipient a 'Happy Birthday' or merely conveyed 'Birthday Greetings'. In every sense of the word, they were prosaic. Though they were illustrated, the pictures they showed were unrelated to birthdays and were frequently the same as the pictures shown on Christmas cards.

To make them more attractive, some cards were embossed and ornamented with silk fringes around the edges. For some reason, however, the novel cards did not catch on and, indeed, were in so little demand that stationers did not feel it worth their while to display them. They stored them in boxes and customers had to ask for them.

In spite of these unpromising beginnings, birthday cards experienced a rebirth in the twentieth century. Specially designed now, and illustrated for the purpose, they carry voluminous wordings, both in verse and in prose. They range in tone from the sentimental and thoughtful to the frivolous and humorous and are decorated with appropriate pictures and good luck symbols.

Of the early cards only the name remained. The modern 'card' is really a folder, often personalised and specialised and catering for all ages.

Birthday celebrations

Birthday celebrations date back to antiquity, when they often took elaborate forms. The Bible tells how Pharaoh celebrated his birthday by giving a feast for all his servants, reviewing appointments and releasing prisoners.

There was a time when birthdays, far from being times of celebration, were considered occasions of crucial significance fraught with peril. They were thought likely to attract the attention of mischievous spirits, particularly prone to interfere at moments of transition or change. A birthday, then, was a time when one needed the support of all one's family and friends. And this was one of the major reasons for the development of the tradition of the birthday party.

To protect the 'birthday child', people came and conveyed their good wishes. These were not mere stereotyped and conventional words. They were a magic formula and were intended to guard the celebrant from untoward attacks.

A birthday, too, was a new beginning, an opportunity to start afresh, and to eliminate all that had stained the past. Games played on the day were not meant primarily to amuse and entertain the visitors, but to make them participate in a magic ritual designed to ward off the evil spirits. Enjoyment, however, did have some importance. The more the guests enjoyed themselves, the more they would be prepared to support their host.

The modern party, characterised by the joyful sharing of special food, harks back to communal meals of earlier times, which were arranged to strengthen the bond between the individual and the community.

BISTRO

The present-day bistro is a leftover from the Napoleonic era and its wars. It goes back to the occupation of Paris by the allied forces after the emperor's defeat in 1814 and owes its existence—as a name—to a misunderstanding.

Russian Cossacks, who were among these troops, particularly enjoyed Parisian life. They proved good customers of its many cheap cafés whose enterprising owners, like modern touts, to solicit business, took up position in front of their establishments. Whenever a Russian passed by, they stopped him and, unable to speak his tongue, made use of the language of gestures. Mimicking the act of eating, they invited him in for a good feed.

As the men always seemed in a hurry, they wanted to assure them that they would not have to wait long to be served. To do so they had specially learnt the Russian word for 'quick' which, in their French accent, sounded like *veestra*.

Nevertheless, the restaurateurs did not succeed in making themselves properly understood and in this respect their effort misfired. Failing to recognise the mispronounced word as one of their own, the Cossacks imagined that the often repeated *veestra* was the French name of a fast-food restaurant and adopted it as such. Thus, with yet another slight variation, the *bistro* came into existence. It not only survived Napoleon, but achieved what he could never do. It conquered the world to become a meeting place offering relaxation and congenial company.

A varied version of the circumstances depicts the Russians less pleasantly. Displaying their status as victors, they are said to have rushed into the small restaurants, arrogantly demanding to be served a cheap meal—instantly. With a strident voice, they commanded the owner to move 'quickly'—which in their tongue was *veestra*.

Not worrying about, or even aware of, the actual meaning of the Russian word, the café owners adopted it as their name. It was to become the (thus mispronounced) 'bistro'.

Both derivations have been questioned. The bistro, yet a further explanation claims, had nothing to do with the occupation of Paris by foreign troops or the Russian language, however distorted. It merely recalled a cheap drink, known as *bistouille*, served in those bars.

BITE THE BULLET

A person who bites the bullet, without any sign of fear, acts with great courage in the face of adversity.

The phrase recollects a dangerous army practice in the

1850s. Soldiers were then equipped with the British Enfield rifle. Prior to using it, they had to bite off the head of the cartridge to expose the explosive to the spark which would ignite it. The procedure was fraught with peril, particularly so in the heat of battle. It needed firmness and courage, as even the slightest deviation or hesitancy would endanger the soldier. Most likely, Kipling's use of the phrase in *The Light That Failed* popularised it: 'Bite the bullet, old man, and don't let them think you're afraid.'

The very practice is said to have been responsible for the Indian mutiny in 1857. The British had enlisted the Sepoys in their forces. These belonged to the Hindu and Moslem faiths and were renowned for their courage and fortitude. Given the then still novel Enfield rifle, each time when using it they had to bite the bullet. However, they refused to do so—and for a deeply religious reason.

The cartridges were greased, and rumour soon spread that the substances used were tallow and lard, both shunned by devout Hindus and Moslems. Nobody could force them to put those ritually defiled cartridges near their lips! Hindus worship the cow, the source of tallow, and no Moslem would touch lard, obtained from the pig.

Out of loyalty to their religion, the Sepoys therefore disobeyed orders, for which reason they were imprisoned by the British. The action caused not only upheaval but, ultimately, resulted in rebellion. Liberated by their fellow religionists, the Sepoys joined forces with them to throw off the foreign yoke. They massacred Europeans and marched to Delhi, to proclaim there the Mogul emperor. The rest is history.

Military in origin as well, but totally different in association, is another derivation of the phrase. This links the 'biting of the bullet' with the attempt to save the lives of seriously wounded soldiers. Realising the necessity to amputate one of their limbs, and with anaesthetics unavailable on the battlefield, the surgeon made the injured man bite on a bullet. It helped him to give vent to his anguish and to withstand pain almost beyond endurance.

BITING REMARKS

A 'biting remark' might hurt, though no one would take it literally. An actual incident in classical times has been quoted as the source of the expression. It links it with Zeno, a Greek philosopher of the fifth century BC, who also was a political activist.

Having failed in a conspiracy to depose the local tyrant, he was arrested and condemned to a torturous end. He was to be pounded to death in a mortar.

The execution was carried out in the very presence of the man whom, for the good of the community, he had sought to destroy. While suffering the protracted agony of his death, as it were with his dying breath, Zeno told the tyrant that he was now willing, and anxious indeed, to reveal to him some secret, significant piece of information.

The dictator could not resist. To make sure he was able to hear what Zeno had to say, he bent over to listen to what now had become a mere whisper, and put his ear close to the philosopher's mouth. This was exactly what Zeno had expected. With his last strength, he bit off the tyrant's ear!

Zeno's 'biting remark' not only left its mark on this enemy of the people, but has survived the millennia, even if only as a metaphor used for sarcasm.

BLACKBALL

Anyone 'blackballed' is excluded from a club, a society or a Masonic Lodge. The description can be taken very literally. It originated in a simple democratic way of voting.

Those entitled to participate in the decision indicated their approval or rejection by means of a ball they placed into a box. A white ball signified their affirmation, and a black one their disapproval. It was an unmistakable way of saying yes or no.

Generally, the colour of the maximum number of balls cast, determined the preferred candidate or agreed upon policy. Anyone not wanted by the majority and thus rejected was therefore 'blackballed'. In some societies and lodges, the presence of even a single black ball was sufficient to deny admittance.

The use of black balls can be traced to ancient Rome. The first-century BC poet, Ovid, in his *Metamorphoses* (XV,41), recalls the custom as it was then applied in the judicial system. An accused person was condemned by black balls, but acquitted by white ones.

Though modern methods of casting votes no longer make use of an actual ball, it is still retained—literally—in the *ball*ot, in spite of the ball now taking the form of a sheet of paper.

BLACK BOOK OR BLACKLISTED

Black has always been a forbidding colour, darkening people's character and life. Negative in its connotation, it is inseparably linked with the Black Death, the blackguard, the black sheep and blackbirding. Melancholy was once thought to be the result of black bile, and English judges used to don a black cap when passing a death sentence. It is no wonder therefore that people under suspicion, known to have a criminal record, or having failed to pay their debts were 'blacklisted'.

Black books then superseded the black list and, in keeping with their name (or being responsible for it, according to some authorities), were bound in black leather covers.

Among the earliest black lists were those compiled by order of King Henry VIII (in the 1530s). In his fight against the church, he issued instructions to have a record made of all religious institutions, described as centres of 'manifest sin, vicious, carnal and abominable living'. When the compilation was completed, it was bound in black covers, for which reason it became known as the 'black book'. The king cleverly used it to have a bill passed in parliament (in March 1536) which decreed the closure of all monasteries and the confiscation of their property, for 'His Majesty [to] have and enjoy' all their possessions.

Thus the 'black book', most likely, became part of the English vocabulary, as it were by royal decree. It did not die with the dissolution of the monasteries, but was found useful in many ways.

Another historic black list goes back to Charles II who, on his ascendance to the throne (in 1661), recorded the names of the men held most responsible for his late father's execution, to have them apprehended and duly punished.

Other well-known examples of black lists belong to illustrious institutions of learning, such as the universities of Oxford and Cambridge. Students who had disgraced their college by some misdemeanour had their names entered in them, with the result that they were barred from taking a degree. Soldiers who had disobeyed orders equally had their names so listed.

The records are now merely a matter of history or exhibits in archives and museums. But we still speak of a person to be shunned or even to be kept out of a society or company as being 'blacklisted'. Not so long ago, prior to the introduction of computers, immigration officers at ports of entry of many a country would look up a large book bound in black covers to check whether the traveller's name was in it. If so, they were refused admission.

From its literal application in varied circumstances, the black book left its mark in idiomatic language. Anyone in one's black book, figuratively speaking, is out of favour, in disgrace.

BLACK DAYS

A 'black day' owes its description to its lack of anything to brighten it up. It is a day that has been spoiled by bad luck or by some disastrous event. History records many such days, some of them commemorating financial disasters such as the devastating stock market crash that preceded the Great Depression.

BLARNEY

Meaningless, flattering talk is 'blarney'. It is one of the few words royalty has added to ordinary people's vocabulary. Its birthplace is the famous Irish castle of that name.

Situated 10 kilometres (6 miles) north of Cork, it was built in 1446 by Cormac MacCarthy, the Earl of Blarney. A bastion, its walls extend to a height of 26 metres (28 yards) and are almost four metres thick at their base.

Legend tells that when in 1602 the English had encircled the castle after a prolonged siege its lord agreed to hand it over 'presently'. In a personal letter to Queen Elizabeth I, in the most flowery language, he vowed his future allegiance to the English crown, reiterating the promise of his immediate evacuation of the stronghold. However, when the date agreed upon arrived, he found an excuse to delay it. This happened not merely once but many a time. When the queen heard of yet another such postponement, worded as before in a long rambling letter, she remarked, 'This is Blarney. What he says he never means.' It was the birth of the word.

Traditionally, the earl had acquired his eloquence and the ability to say sweet nothing in ever so many words— supernaturally. Kissing one specific stone which has been incorporated in the parapet of the castle miraculously had bestowed on him the gift and—still identified—has been known worldwide ever since as the 'Blarney Stone'.

BLAZE A TRAIL

A trailblazer derives this laudatory name from those who preceded as pioneers in the field of exploration. Now a mere metaphor, initially it referred to an actual practice of earlier pathfinders. To enable those following them to find their way in the still uncharted wooded territory, they marked the trees along their trail. They did so by chipping off some of the bark. The lighter patches this created served as signposts and were known as 'blazes'.

The word 'blaze' is derived from the German *Blesse*, used for a 'white marking'. Originally, it was applied to a white spot on an animal's forehead and in its etymology goes back to a root that meant 'to shine'.

A wealth of tradition is thus contained in an explorer's 'blazing of a trail'.

BLOW HOT AND COLD

People who vacillate in their opinions and quickly change from being enthusiastic to showing disinterest are said to 'blow hot and cold'.

The saying can be traced to one of Aesop's *Fables*. This tells of an encounter between a wayfarer and a satyr, the Greek woodland deity portrayed as a human with animal features.

It was a cold winter's day, and the freezing traveller was blowing on his stiff fingers. Mystified, the satyr wanted to know what he was doing. The man explained to him that with his breath he was warming his chilled fingers.

Taking pity on him, the satyr invited the man to his home for a hot meal. This time, he watched him blowing on the food, which intrigued him all the more. Inquiring why he did so, his guest explained that he was blowing on the stew to cool it down.

The satyr told the traveller to leave at once. He was not prepared to entertain or ever mix with anyone who could 'blow hot and cold from the same mouth'.

BLOW ONE'S TOP

Anyone 'blowing their top' does much more than just letting off steam. They almost explode in their frustration and anger, releasing pent-up feelings. A most apposite phrase, it comes straight from nature and the frightening experience of a volcano, which erupts through pressure built up inside by gases and steam, literally blowing its top—sometimes with devastating effect.

A phrase borrowed from vulcanology, it has been applied to many other and varied situations of life and death. It has been linked with a raging storm at sea causing the loss—the 'blowing out'—of a topsail. Jazz music, crude sex and modern drug culture, too, have made use of the idiom. Last but not least, suicides blowing out their brains with a gun blow their top.

Blow a raspberry

To 'give (or blow) a raspberry' leaves no doubt that the person so treated is held in contempt and not wanted. As it were, they are hissed off the stage or, in American terminology, given the Bronx cheer. A rude sound, it is easily produced by putting the tongue between closed lips and then forcibly expelling air through the mouth. No one could mistake it, and nothing could be more effective in showing disapproval.

Obviously, the sound imitates the breaking of wind. Its description as a raspberry has nothing to do with the fruit but rather comes from rhyming slang. Rhyming slang, according to some authorities, did not originate, as sometimes suggested, merely as a light-hearted entertainment among the lower classes. English cockneys are said to have invented it to mystify and annoy Irish migrants who, working alongside them, were employed in the building of English railways and canals.

In typical rhyming slang a word or name is replaced by another one or a phrase with which it rhymes. By such method, the speaker avoids mentioning what or whom they really have in mind. To make it still more difficult, if not impossible for those ignorant of the code, even to guess it, they use merely the first part of the phrase chosen as a substitute.

'Apples and pears' thus stands for 'stairs'; 'four by twos' referred to 'Jews' and 'elephant's trunk' spoke of someone as being 'drunk'.

The alert Irish were not slow in catching on and created their own type of rhyming slang. Criminals, too, soon realised the usefulness of such code and created a jargon all of their own.

This ingenious method was responsible for the raspberry as well. The common and unmentionable 'fart' was substituted with 'raspberry tart'. Dropping eventually the second rhyming giveaway word, all that was left was the fruity part. Consequently, the raspberry, on its own, most respectably took the place of the objectionable and vulgar allusion to people's loss of control at one end of their anatomy.

BLUDGER

Those who would rather live on the dole than work, in Australian English are contemptuously called 'bludgers'. The term was first applied to pimps who, shirking work, lived from prostitutes' earnings, documented as early as 1882.

The name is not original but comes from the bludgeoners who, to get their own way and obtain all they wanted, knocked down people with a bludgeon, a short stout club. In modern usage, the bludger has changed into a much more gentle sort of person, suffering from an allergy to work.

BLUE MONDAY

A busy weekend, with all the enjoyment that goes with it, is frequently followed by its anticlimax, the 'blue Monday'.

The choice of blue was not accidental. It is based on the old misconception that those who overindulged in drink saw, apart from the proverbial 'pink elephants', blue devils as well. They imagined everything to be 'discoloured' by a bluish tint. Even after they had sobered up, the blue devils seemed to stay on, colouring the person's mood and giving rise to the expression 'the blues'.

Historically, the blue Monday may go back to one particular day of the year—the Monday preceding the abstemious season of Lent. Aware that a prolonged period of deprivation lay ahead, people, as it were, had a last fling. The clergy approved of this and, to mark the day, had the churches decorated with blue drapes. Very appropriately, then, the day was designated as 'blue Monday'.

As worshippers were exempted from certain tasks on that day, its colour became identified as well with a general reluctance to work. When, however, people became too unruly, as a result of excessive drinking and fasting, the church authorities abolished the holiday. But memories of its celebration preserved 'blue Monday' in our vocabulary.

BOB'S YOUR UNCLE

'Bob's your uncle' is an assurance that all will be well and that there is no need to worry. Someone of influence or authority will look after you.

Several figures have been suggested as the original Bob. Pride of place, no doubt, belongs to Sir Robert Peel's 'bobbies'. Parents assured their children that there was no cause for them ever to be scared when alone in the street. They could always go up to a policeman, known in England as a bobby. He was like one of the family. In fact, 'Bob's your uncle'!

Less flattering is another derivation. It links the phrase with the appointment in 1887 of Arthur Balfour as chief secretary for Ireland. Balfour was chosen for the position by the prime minister at the time, Robert Gascoyne, the Marquis of Salisbury. This 'Bob' was Balfour's uncle! The appointment was a case of nepotism, and was apparently a profitable relationship.

It may also be possible that no person was involved at all in the creation of the phrase, but that it developed from an old slang expression in which 'all is bob' was used for 'all is safe'.

BONKERS

Originally, anyone 'bonkers', in the language of slang, was slightly 'drunk'. No doubt, their strange demeanour eventually led people to think they were crazy. Eric Partridge, in fact, suggested that the word might be derived from a knock on a person's head. The 'bonk' on the 'bonce', colloquially speaking, had affected the brain.

BRAND NEW

If an object is described as brand new, people might wrongly assume that it is so called because it is entirely new on the market, something not produced before. On the other hand, they might imagine that it is meant to indicate that the article has never been used and consequently still clearly displays the brand name of the maker.

Though feasible, these suggestions do not explain the origin of the term. In Old English, a brand was a torch or a flame responsible for the 'fire brand'. Anything brand new therefore referred to an object, mostly of metal, that had just come out of the fiery furnace. In this sense Shakespeare spoke of 'fire-new fortune', 'a man of fire-new words' and fire-new from the mint'.

The brand, as it were, plucked out of the fire, has long been extinguished. Nonetheless, it is still being used for anything that is absolutely new, which is praised and promoted as 'brand new'.

BRIDESMAIDS AND GROOMSMEN

For bridal couples to be accompanied at their wedding by bridesmaids and groomsmen is a custom which goes back to ancient Roman nuptials. To be properly solemnised and legally recognised necessitated the presence of ten witnesses. These were the original bridesmaids and groomsmen.

When circumstances changed and this quorum of witnesses was no longer needed, their presence had become redundant. Nevertheless, though now reduced in number, some of them, as it were, stayed on to become attendants of the bride and groom.

They came to play a new, and perhaps much more significant role, at a time when superstition ran riot. People were afraid of jealous forces which they were convinced were out to destroy happiness and particularly that of a couple about to become husband and wife.

A bride and groom therefore felt specially threatened on their wedding day. They imagined that evil spirits were determined to do them harm and destroy their marital bliss. It was for this reason that the couple invited their best friends to accompany them—as groomsmen and bridesmaids. Their presence was meant to confuse the nefarious force as to the identity of the bride and the groom. For this purpose they matched the clothes they wore to those of the couple. Not sure who was who, the evil forces gave up the pursuit to turn elsewhere. The groomsmen and bridesmaids thus had taken on the task of acting as decoys. Bride and groom could be at ease, no longer having to worry about the devil spoiling their day and their future happiness.

When such fears of potential magic evil no longer existed, groomsmen and bridesmaids had lost their function to serve as a source of confusion. For the second time, they had become superfluous. But just as when their role as witnesses had lapsed, they were still retained as members of the wedding party. New duties allotted to them, in reality, are merely an excuse to explain their (unnecessary) presence.

BRING DOWN THE HOUSE

Tumultuous applause is described as 'bringing down the house'. This present-day metaphor, in its original setting, applied very literally. It goes back to the time when travelling theatre companies staged their shows in ramshackle buildings, barns or makeshift tents. The boisterous acclamation of an overenthusiastic audience could result in the collapse of the wonky structure.

BROWBEAT

Some people are easily intimidated. They can be discouraged even without a single word being spoken. A mere gesture can make them conform or stop them from doing something. Using body language, the dominant party merely has to frown—to wrinkle the brow, to 'browbeat' the victim into submission.

BROWNED OFF

To be browned off uses a somewhat colourful phrase in a sombre hue to express one's being totally fed up and disheartened.

London cockneys are said to have been responsible for it. They used to call a penny (the later 'copper') a 'brown'. They were 'browned off' when people gave them a penny to go away and stop bothering them.

A popular slang expression in the British army during the Second World War, it is sometimes said to have originated among the soldiers themselves. Bored by their endless routine marches, it seemed to them that their mind had become rusty, the rust figuratively staining them with its brown colour. Truly, they were 'browned off'.

An apocryphal story traces the origin of the idiom to a member of the Suffolk Regiment when stationed in Singapore in 1927. During a route march, the commanding officer, dissatisfied with the soldiers' performance, strongly reprimanded them. One of the men, with typical British humour, though under his breath still very audibly, remarked to his comrades, 'He is blacked-off, but we are all browned-off'.

His colourful aside had been suggested by the tan of their faces acquired during their ceaseless marches in the hot tropical sun. With their home in England, they were not used to being exposed to it.

The private's comment did not no unheard or unheeded. In fact, it has never been forgotten, as it has become part of the English language.

BRUMBY

There are two explanations as to how the brumby, the Australian wild horse, received its name.

One explanation is that it is from an Aboriginal root, being derived from *booramby*, meaning 'wild'.

Others assert that the horse is named after Major James Brumby, a member of the New South Wales Corps in the 1790s. He arrived in the colony as a private soldier and became a wealthy pastoralist. Even while still serving in the army, he took up breeding horses on a grant of land which extended over an area of 100 acres (40 ha). Unable to dispose of the animals when transferred to Tasmania (then Van Diemen's Land), he turned them loose to fend for themselves. Running wild, they were soon referred to by the people as Brumby's horses, eventually to be dubbed briefly as brumbies.

Their name was popularised, indeed perpetuated, by one of Banjo Paterson's poems. An incident which occurred at a trial at the Supreme Court of New South Wales prompted him to write it. During the proceedings, reference was made to a 'brumby horse', a description which baffled the presiding judge. He was anxious to know 'Who is Brumby, and where is his run?'

His inspiration fired, Paterson—poetically—gave his explanation in 'Brumby's Run'. He portrayed Brumby as the owner of a 'station' in the vast area of the still unsettled outback 'beyond the Western Pines' with wild horses—his only stock—roaming about free.

BUCKLEY'S CHANCE

Having Buckley's chance, a typical Australianism, means to have little or no chance at all. It is a phrase mainly used in a negative sense. Several suggestions have been made as to who this (unlucky) individual was.

One tradition identifies him with William Buckley, a convict. Accused of having received a roll of cloth he knew to have been stolen, he had been transported from England 'for life'. However, in 1803, he succeeded in escaping from Port Phillip.

No one believed that he would be able to stay free for long and survive. He just had no chance. But Buckley proved otherwise. For 32 years he lived in the bush, where Aborigines adopted this 'wild white man' in the belief that he was the reincarnation of their dead tribal chief.

Several times people claimed to have caught sight of this giant of a man (he was 6 feet, 6 inches tall—1.95 metres), long-bearded and wrapped in kangaroo skins. It was only in 1835 that Buckley surrendered to a party led by the surveyor and explorer John Wedge, who recommended (and obtained) his pardon. So long separated from his countrymen, Buckley could no longer converse in English, which it took him some time to master again.

Another contestant for being 'the' Buckley was Richard Buckley, a murderer. While holding up—in the 1890s—the Glenferry Bank in Victoria, he shot dead its manager, Mr Berriman. Though for some considerable time he succeeded in eluding the law, he had no chance to do so indefinitely. Run down eventually, he was arrested. Almost miraculously for this period, he was not hanged. Kept in custody, he was released only when an old man.

The third Mr Buckley possibly recalled in the phrase was a totally different sort of a person, a business magnate in his time. He was Mars Buckley. In 1851, he established a Melbourne firm with Crumpton Nunn as his partner. The business which developed into one of the earliest department stores of Australia became known as 'Buckley & Nunn'.

Australians, loving rhyming slang, welcomed the new business venture as a wonderful opportunity to enrich the store of their language. Soon they referred to the hopelessness of a case by a pun on the firm's name. 'There are just two chances, Buckley's and none,' they said.

BUGS AND BUGGING

Hidden microphones used in modern spying colloquially are referred to as 'bugs' as, in their early stage, the models of this electronic device, with their protruding aerials, looked very much like insects.

Possibly, the bug may even go back to the world of the occult. Ghosts haunting and harming people were known as bugs, a name derived from the Welsh *bwg* for an evil and mischievous spirit. Invisible to the ordinary eye, it watched and followed its victims, waiting for its moment to prey upon them.

The 'bug' interfering with modern computers is said to have received its description from this ghostly being as well. However, a natural derivation claims that it recalls the early days of computers when insects crawling into them created havoc.

BUTTONHOLE

To 'buttonhole' someone means to detain them, in most cases as an involuntary listener. The term makes little sense. It has no connection with a buttonhole—whether the actual hole in a coat lapel or the flower pinned to it. It is all a mistake and the result of one wrong letter, the buttonhole's final 'e'. Whoever corners the unlucky person gets hold of one of their buttons. Not to let them go, they button hold them.

BUTTONHOLE WORN AT A WEDDING

Grooms and groomsmen traditionally wear a 'buttonhole', also known by the French *boutonnière*. It contributes to their festive appearance. What they do not usually realise is that the flower pinned to their lapels is a relic of the early days of men's dress and used to have a magic purpose.

In Anglo-Saxon times buttons were unknown. Instead of 'buttoning up' their coats, men fastened them by means of a ribbon which they pulled through holes in the lapel introduced for this very purpose.

At weddings, the knot they tied was believed to play an additional magical role. Apart from securing the garment around the neck, much more significantly it was thought to act as a love charm. Supernaturally, it tied the knot of the marriage bond, for husband and wife to stay together for the rest of their lives.

Jackets have buttons now and therefore no longer need ribbons. Though redundant, the 'buttonhole' and its ribbon have been retained, transformed into a flower. Taking the place of the original love knot, unbeknown to the wedding party, the 'buttonhole' casts its own spell with all the other magic paraphernalia of the nuptials.

BY AND LARGE

Public speakers and, not least so, politicians, when explaining a theory or a policy, frequently use the expression 'by and large' instead of the much more intelligible 'on the whole' or 'generally speaking'. They are unaware that their choice of words, admitting that their statement is imprecise, originally was a naval term. Appropriately, those using 'by and large' should thus be described as being 'at sea'.

In the days of sailing, the man at the helm had to pay careful attention whether to sail the vessel *on* or close to (*off*) the wind. The order 'full and by' directed him to sail as close *to* the wind as was possible, keeping the sails *full* of wind. On the other hand, asked to do so merely 'by and large' meant that he was to sail near to (in fact, slightly off) the wind, but not fully on it. It was a much easier manoeuvre.

Now totally divorced from the sea, 'by and large' continues to suggest a lack of exactitude. It is a mere approximation.

By-laws

By-laws are laws issued by local authorities. The word literally says so, as 'by' (or 'bye') perpetuates the Old Norse word for 'dwelling place' or a 'town'. By-laws therefore, as distinct from the general laws which applied to the entire country or realm, concerned the smaller communities. They were regulations issued and enacted by the city council, the corporation or the borough.

Many an English town originally established by the Danes retains its founder's language in the final ending of its name. Rug*by*, Whit*by* and Der*by* are typical examples. They all preserve the original Norse 'town'. Derby, for instance, means the 'town on the (river) Derwent'.

Later generations, unaware of the significance of the 'by', misinterpreted it. They believed it not to be a noun but a mere adverb, stating that something was just 'by' the way. It was like a by-pass, in its origin a subsidiary, secondary road.

CAB

CAMOUFLAGE

CAN'T SEE THE WOOD FOR THE TREES

CAR BONNET AND BOOT

CASINO

CATCH–22

CAUGHT WITH ONE'S PANTS DOWN

CHAIRPERSON

CHAMPAGNE GLASS

CHAUVINISM

CHEQUE

CHEQUERED BLACK AND WHITE
FLAG IN MOTOR RACING

CHIPS ARE DOWN

CHOCK-A-BLOCK

CINCH

CLEAN AS A WHISTLE

CLINK

COACH

COASTERS AND WHY THE PORT IS
PASSED FROM RIGHT TO LEFT

COAT OF ARMS

COCK-AND-BULL STORY

COCKNEYS

CODSWALLOP

COLD ENOUGH TO FREEZE THE BALLS
OFF A BRASS MONKEY

COME A CROPPER

COME TO A HEAD

COOL ONE'S HEELS

COPPER

COTTON ON

CRANKY

CROWBAR

CROW'S NEST

CRYING OUT LOUD

CURFEW

CUT AND DRIED

Cab

The cab is a shortened 'goat'—as a word at least.

First built in Italy, in the late eighteenth century, originally it was a horse-drawn two-wheeled vehicle, light in weight and well sprung. With roads still uneven and rough, it enabled passengers to have a comparatively smooth ride, no longer being jolted about by so many bumps. Imaginatively, the inventors therefore compared their novel vehicle's run with the capering of a young goat. In fact, they called their carriage after it—*capri-ola*. (*Caper* in Latin is a goat.)

It did not take long for the French to adopt the new carriage. Adapting its name to their tongue, it became known as a *cabriole*, a word replaced by its diminutive, *cabriolet*.

Realising the great advantage of the coach, the British took it over from the French. They officially introduced the cabriolet as a public vehicle on 23 April 1823. The date was specially chosen. It was the king's birthday and the launching of the new service provided a unique opportunity of celebrating the occasion. Cleverly, fares charged were one-third less than those by the hackney coaches. Indeed, it was like a royal birthday present to the people.

Always practical, the English soon cut down the name of the cabriolet, changing it into the modern 'cab'.

Cynics have been less kind in explaining the description. They suggested the passengers chose it because the new contraption bounced and knocked them about so much that they could well imagine being carried along not in a coach, but on the back of a wild, frisky goat!

Camouflage

Camouflage is both a natural phenomenon and a military expedient.

Nature has endowed certain species with colours or features that make them blend in with their environment. It prevents predators from spotting them. Some creatures—like the chameleon—for the purpose of self-protection, are even able to change colour.

Man, as in so many ways, has imitated nature and applied its wisdom to situations he has to confront, not least so, in warfare. To conceal his presence from the enemy, he learnt to disguise his encampments, engines of war, and himself, by adopting the colouration and conspicuous features of the territory he occupied or had to traverse in the circumstances.

Referred to as camouflage, the term is derived from the French *camouflet*, 'a puff of smoke'. Obviously, and no matter what form it takes nowadays, it recalls the use of a smoke screen to be invisible from hostile forces.

CAN'T SEE THE WOOD
FOR THE TREES

The well-known phrase that 'you can't see the wood for the trees' has been traced to an English proverb first recorded in 1546. Obviously, it applied to a person who, by paying too much attention to a mass of details, fails to appreciate the true value and meaning of an object or situation. They lose sight of the real issue by concentrating too much on non-essential minutiae.

Another interpretation suggests that you can't see the wood (i.e. the forest—the total view) because you are preoccupied with a single tree close at hand.

The observation was popularised by Christoph Martin Wieland, an eighteenth-century German writer. He used it in one of his works in 1768, more than a century after it had been quoted in Britain. He based the simile on a French story of 1682, which had appeared in several German versions. It related the experience of a young gentleman on his first visit to Paris. He had been told that he would see a large and beautiful city. However, to his great disappointment he saw nothing of it. The many houses had obscured his view!

CAR BONNET AND BOOT

The bonnet of a car is so called because—like a hat—it protects the engine. In order to stand out and attract attention, car manufacturers used to decorate their bonnet by some distinctive feature. The boot, belonging to the other end of both the body and the car, can be traced to two different sources.

To begin with, it was a simple box containing luggage and other items, which was placed at the back of the car. A box is *boîte* in French. The English appropriated the custom and the word, Anglicising the latter into 'boot'.

In the days of horse-drawn vehicles, members of the English upper class employed footmen known as 'boots', so called because their many domestic duties included the polishing of their masters' boots. They accompanied their masters on trips. It was their job then to assist them to get in and out of the coach which, with the passengers' cabin high above the ground, necessitated some stepping up and down.

During the journey, the footmen took their place at the rear of the carriage, standing on a platform provided for them. It did not take long for this to be called by their 'title'—'boot'.

Though this former place of the 'boot' (of either kind) is now covered and occupied by luggage and other paraphernalia, it retains its original, though now no longer applicable, name. Once created in English class society, it persists as a moving memorial of the now obsolete footmen.

Americans, always to the point, have updated the terms by calling the bonnet a hood and the boot a trunk.

Casino

Universally, a public place for gambling is known as a casino.
And yet, its designation makes no mention of its function.
From the Italian, *casino* solely means 'a little house', the
diminutive of *casa*.

Catch–22

Modern times and literature have given us 'Catch–22' as a
most concise description of the paradoxical situation in
which whoever is caught in it, has no way out.

The American author Joseph Heller vividly described such a
dilemma and gave it its name, using it as the title of a
satirical novel, first published in 1961. A best-seller, its title
and very problem soon caught the attention of the public and
'Catch–22', a predicament well understood, became part of
our language.

After having participated in numerous bombing missions,
an American airman in the Second World War felt the need to
be relieved from further duties. However, when asking not to
be rostered for more flights, he was informed that, according
to regulations, permission to stop flying could only be
granted if he could prove insanity. The mere fact that he
asked to be excused from going on any more dangerous
flights proved that, far from being crazy, he was very sane
indeed! He had reached a deadlock.

Actually, to call the excruciating predicament 'Catch–22'
was merely a second choice. Originally, Heller had referred to
it as 'Catch–18'. However, as Leon Uris' book *Mila 18* had just
come on to the market, the publishers felt it wise to change
Heller's title at the last moment. To use the identical number
would have led to confusion and served neither author.
Luckily, to solve this problem presented no extra hitch!

CAUGHT WITH ONE'S PANTS DOWN

A person who is caught with their pants down is taken completely by surprise. The result depends on the circumstances. Whichever way, they expose themselves and are placed in an awkward and unenviable position—risking life or, at the very least, reputation.

The saying is of doubtful parentage. According to one suggestion, it stems from the American wild west and frontier days. It so happened that an American Indian caught sight of a white man just when he was relieving himself. With his trousers down, he did not have his firearm at the ready and, therefore, totally unprepared for the encounter, became an easy target.

More general and up-to-date is another explanation. It relates the phrase to the compromising situation—when a wife catches her husband with his pants off—enjoying illicit sex with another woman!

CHAIRPERSON

With women's liberation, the chairperson has replaced the now obsolete chairman. Paradoxically, the title—even in its gender neutralised version—has been outdated for many years.

Totally meaningless nowadays, if taken literally, the term made good sense centuries ago when it was first applied. Chairs then were still uncommon. Being rare, they were expensive. Those attending meetings were seated on rough benches. Only the person presiding, out of respect to the office and position, occupied a chair. Possibly, it was the only one available. That made that person (and very conspicuously so) the 'chairman', and anyone who spoke of or to them could not be misunderstood when addressing (or referring to) 'the chair', by calling them 'Mr Chairman'. When women eventually came to hold the office as well, they were addressed as 'Madam Chairman', a contradictory combination.

Everyone now sits on a chair and so, logically, all those attending a meeting should be called chairpersons. But this would defeat the purpose of the choice of title. Habits of the past, even when they have become obsolete and meaningless, are not discarded, nor do terms and practices they created. Retained as a relic of the past, the chairperson, as it were, has become a fixture.

CHAMPAGNE GLASS

It is said that the saucer-shape of a champagne glass, commonly used nowadays, is the result of a love affair. It was modelled on a woman's breast—that of Madame Pompadour, mistress of King Louis XV of France.

The shape, in spite of its alleged romantic association, is the least suitable for the full enjoyment of the drink, in no small measure due to its bubbles. The extended width of the glass contributes to their rapid dissipation and thereby greatly reduces the pleasure. No wonder that the original champagne glass was narrow-brimmed, which gave the bubbles a much longer time to rise!

Another of its conspicuous early features was its hollow stem. It, too, had a practical reason, though now obsolete. When wine was not as refined as it is today, it allowed the dregs to settle in the hollow stem and for people to enjoy a pure drink.

Chauvinism

Currently chauvinism is almost exclusively associated with sexism. Forgotten is its original use as the description of extreme patriotism. It became such by a strange combination of circumstances. But for a stage play, it would never have existed.

It goes back to Napoleonic times, and one of the emperor's soldiers, Nicolas Chauvin. He had distinguished himself in many battles, being wounded, as the story has it, 17 times. In recognition of his services, Napoleon himself, it was further told, had presented him with a ceremonial sword and red ribbon, and ensured that he was paid a pension.

Even after the emperor's final defeat, Chauvin continued to worship him and did so in the most exaggerated terms. Demobilised and badly scarred, Chauvin returned to his village. He did not settle down quietly but went about constantly praising his fallen idol. Fanatically, he described him as the greatest hero of all times, and Napoleon was the sole topic of all his conversations. Almost obsessed by his past military career, Chauvin used any and every opportunity to display his patriotism.

It did not take long for him to become a figure of fun. No doubt his name would have been forgotten had not dramatists made him the central figure of their plays. Most notable among them were Charles and Jean Cogniard. They truly immortalised Chauvin in their comedy *La Cocarde Tricolore*, which they wrote in 1831. His protestation of extreme devotion to his country, 'I am French, I am Chauvin', soon caught the imagination of the people. It created chauvinism as a term for blind and excessive patriotism.

CHEQUE

The earliest cheques were bills of exchange. First used in Italy in the thirteenth century, they were then adopted by the Dutch, reaching England in the seventeenth century. The original cheque was payable to the nominated person alone and could not be transferred. The new practice greatly simplified trade, as it no longer necessitated the movement of bullion or other moneys, often over great distances. It enabled the seller even if living in a far-off district to collect the money owed from a local trader.

Typical is one of the earliest English cheques still in existence. It is in the way of a letter dated 16 August 1675 and addressed to a Mr Thomas Fowles, a goldsmith in Fleet Street, London. It instructed him 'to pay unto Mr Samuel Howard or order upon receipt hereof the sum of nine pounds thirteene shillings and sixpence'.

The bill of exchange could take many other forms. It could simply be written on a scrap of paper, a piece of cloth or other material or, as is said to have happened at least once, on the hide of a live cow.

Originally spelled 'check', it was named after the counterfoil of a bill used to check the validity of the transaction and to serve as a safeguard against alterations or forgeries. It was only later that the name was transferred to the entire 'document'. The Americans retained its original spelling, whilst the British adopted the French version.

CHEQUERED BLACK AND WHITE FLAG IN MOTOR RACING

Motor racing presents its own thrills and dangers. To avoid fatal accidents and collisions, it necessitates careful supervision and meticulous organisation. For this purpose, the *Fédération Internationale de l'Automobile*, as the controlling body of the sport, has introduced a worldwide system of (altogether) eighteen signals. In the form of flags, these are designed in patterns that can easily be memorised and recognised by the drivers. Proceeding at record speeds, and hence catching only a glimpse of the signal when approaching it, they must be able to identify it in a split second and against any background. A mistake made in 'reading' the message can cost them the race, if not their life!

Each flag relates to a specific circumstance or emergency. The variety of situations includes the need to stop instantly (obviously conveyed by a red flag), the approach of some dangerous stretch (yellow), information that oil covers the course further along the track (yellow with red stripes) or that an ambulance is ahead (a white flag). But nothing is more significant to those taking part than the end of the race, hopefully the 'winning post'. To make the flag indicating it truly outstanding and distinct from all the others, it is the only one which is chequered, with black-and-white squares. So different, no one could ever mistake it. Traditionally, it should only be waved for the winning car, while it is held steady for all the rest.

CHIPS ARE DOWN

Life has been likened to a gamble and, indeed, not a few metaphors applying to its various situations have come from the gaming room. Just as on occasions one has to 'go back to square one' or is 'checkmated', so it is said of a moment of crisis or testing that 'the chips are down'. The chips represent the money bets at poker. When all the chips have been placed, the players have to reveal their cards and, at this exciting moment, the winning hand is discovered.

Chock-a-block

Nautical terminology and experience are the basis of calling anything crammed to capacity, with no empty space left, 'chock-a-block' full. It relates to a situation when the running and standing blocks of a tackle are so close together that they cannot be moved. Quite literally, they are 'blocked'.

The chock in the phrase is a 'block of wood' or a 'wedge'. Etymologically it can be traced back to at least the fourteenth century and a root that described the 'jaw bone'. Chock-full has been explained as 'full to the chops', so much so that it was choking one.

Cinch

To say of something easily accomplished that 'it's a cinch' uses the Spanish word *cincha*, for a saddle-strap. Two versions explain its choice.

On their conquest of Mexico in 1519, the conquistadors introduced into the country their Spanish horses. In no time these multiplied and ran wild. Mexicans found it very difficult to round them up, which demanded great skill. To make sure that their saddle would not slip and throw them, they ingeniously fastened it with a belly strap, the *cincha*. It gave them a firm grip and thereby facilitated their task which they could now execute without much difficulty or peril to themselves. This 'cinch' thus became synonymous with anything requiring little effort.

Of much later date is a second explanation. This traces the phrase to the Californian gold rush of 1849. Adventurers arriving from the east, even if unsuccessful in digging up gold, picked up a most useful new practice in securing their saddles. Often on horseback all day long in search of the elusive glittering substance, and still using the traditional

English type of saddle, theirs was not a smooth ride. Frequently, they had to stop and dismount to tighten the slipping saddle girth. They noticed that Mexican and Indian riders had solved the problem by using their own kind of belly band; a rope they made of twisted horse hair. This not only stayed in place, but was not difficult to adjust. Keeping the saddle in position throughout, it made the ride an 'easy thing'. *Cincha*, the Spanish word for this equine girth, thus became part of the language used to describe anything that was as 'easy and sure' as being secured by a cinch.

CLEAN AS A WHISTLE

To make a pure sound, a whistle has to be completely clean. No dirt or saliva must block it. For anything to be 'as clean as [such] a whistle' became a favourite metaphor among writers. Instead of speaking of it as being clean, they might refer to it as being clear, pure and dry, or as Robert Burns did, as 'empty'.

Definite and clear in its sound, it is no wonder that 'clean as a whistle' became a simile for anything that was unsullied and so intelligible that no one could mistake it.

There are other interpretations as well. It has been claimed that originally the saying did not mention a whistle at all. It referred to a piece of wood that had been carefully shaved or whittled, which gave it an immaculate, spotless look. This made people speak of anything 'as clean as a whittle'. Unfortunately, by slovenly speech the word itself became soiled and that is how the whittle was changed into a whistle!

A further suggestion gives the phrase a martial origin. It recalls the clear whistling sound made by a sword. Wielded fast, it cuts the air in one clean swoop, inflicting an equally 'clean' wound.

CLINK

To refer to prison as 'clink' goes back to at least the sixteenth century and a gaol so called in the London borough of Southwark. John Stow, the famous English chronicler living at the time, was the first to mention it. He relates how it served to incarcerate 'such as should brabble, frey, or break the peace on the said Bank(side), or in the brothel-houses'.

Burnt down in 1780 by the 'No Popery' rioters, it has never been rebuilt. Nevertheless, the street in which it once was situated is still called after it, and its very name survives whenever people speak of the clink.

No doubt its name recalled the sharp loud noise made whenever the cell doors were slammed shut and the rattling of the iron chains with which the prisoners were shackled.

COACH

The coach perpetuates the village of Kocs, situated in northwestern Hungary, in which the first vehicle of its kind was built. Unmatched in comfort and mobility at the time, it was soon adopted all over Europe where, in acknowledgment of the site of its origin, it was referred to as 'the wagon of Kocs'. Anglicised, it became the (modern) coach.

One of the most illustrious Hungarian kings, Matthias Corvinus (1458–90), is said to have been responsible for its construction. Fighting many wars, he had vanquished the Turks, conquered Bohemia and captured Vienna. His, indeed, had become the most powerful kingdom of Europe. Not only a soldier, he equally excelled in the pursuit of culture. A patron of the arts and sciences, he founded the University of Budapest and established a library which became renowned as the finest in Europe.

Visiting many parts of his empire, he was shaken about in

the vehicles put at his disposal. Apart from being totally unsatisfactory in their performance, he felt, they were completely unworthy of his status.

Aware of the craftsmanship of the people of Kocs, he commanded them to construct an up-to-date carriage which embodied every feature to ensure a fast ride in comfort.

When the finished product was presented to him, the four-wheeled vehicle exceeded all his expectations. Nothing like it existed at the time. Its passenger cabin, suspended by leather straps, provided a ride so smooth that even on the roughest of roads the traveller would not be jolted. Sitting in an enclosed compartment, he was protected against weather and wind.

In every place it called, people admired the novel, luxurious carriage. Soon the noble and rich, always anxious to emulate the royal example, had like vehicles built for themselves. Wherever they travelled, they carried the name of the village of its birth. Thus, 'the carriage of Kocs' conquered the roads and made the name of a formerly unknown township world-famous—in its English pronunciation—as 'coach'.

Once a luxury item, it became the generally adopted vehicle and its name was retained in the motorised carriage, to be adopted also as a term for the individual carriages of a train.

COASTERS AND WHY THE PORT IS PASSED FROM RIGHT TO LEFT

Coasters nowadays put under glasses or bottles to protect the table or cloth from being scratched or soiled no longer live up to their name. The original coaster served a different purpose, and there was a valid reason for its being so called.

Not cheap cardboard pads, they were expensively made, often of wood or metal, with a base of cloth or felt. They were part of every elegant home.

After the meal, once the table was cleared and its cloth removed, the port was served. This practice followed a strictly adhered-to ritual. After a guest had filled their glass, they would slide the bottle to their neighbour on the left. To avoid the highly polished table from being scratched, the bottle was placed on a base—to coast along. It was this consideration and practice which was responsible for the coaster and its name.

There was also a reason for the direction the bottle was passed on—clockwise from right to left. It was not a haphazard choice. It followed the movement of the sun, imagined to bring about good fortune!

The term 'to coast' has its own story, going back to an early American winter sport. Both in the United States and in Canada people enjoyed wintry days by sliding down iced-up slopes on sledges. These they referred to as 'coasts', a name then applied to the gliding movement itself in which the rider just sat tight on their sled without any need to propel it.

No wonder that the early 'coasting' was then applied to cyclists who freewheeled down a hill, and to motorists who parsimoniously save petrol on downgrades by turning off the engine.

COAT OF ARMS

Originally, the coat of arms served as a means of recognition that often spelled the difference between life and death, and can be traced back to the twelfth century—particularly to the crusades.

The knights going out to conquer the Holy Land were encased in armour which protected their bodies from head to toe and unless they raised their visor, not even their faces could be seen. As uniforms were still unknown, this made them all look alike, and no one could tell friend from foe.

To distinguish knights in combat, they needed some mark of identification, a device which was their very own. The knight's symbol usually had some link with their family and its past, the service they had rendered to their country or lord, or some individual quality or incident in their life. Conspicuously, they displayed this symbol on the *arm*our they wore, which explains why the design soon became identified with, and known as, their 'arms'. It was shown, too, on the shield and the crest of their helmets.

The burning sun in the Holy Land heated the armour so much that it caused great discomfort to the wearers who, feeling totally exhausted, found it hard to fight. Wisely, they therefore covered their armour with a long flowing cloak of linen or silk, paradoxically, to keep themselves cool (and back home in Europe to protect the armour from rust and dirt). But this, of course, concealed their individual 'armorial bearings' and, still to be recognised, they had these embroidered on their coat which thus became known as their 'coat of arms'.

Modern pursuit of genealogy has renewed interest in a family's coat of arms. After all, if genuine, it bestows special status to its ancestry. Some families, indeed, proudly display their insignia on the gate posts of their homes, their cutlery and even on their stationery.

COCK-AND-BULL STORY

A typical feature of most fables is that all the characters are animals who act and speak like humans. It was first popularised in classical times by the sixth-century B.C. collection of Aesop. They do not represent real life, but literally are cock-and-bull stories, highly imaginative but incredible. This most likely contributed to the description of any unbelievable tale.

Another possible source of the expression were the inns, once a popular centre of social life, each known by a distinctive name, conspicuously displayed on a sign outside. Among the names favoured by the English were 'The Cock' and 'The Bull'. In a jovial mood and high-spirited from their drinks, and not least, to boost their egos, the patrons told all kinds of 'tall tales'. Most of them were of things that had never happened. No wonder that people soon called any fantastic claim, obviously totally untrue, 'a cock-and-bull story'.

COCKNEYS

Correctly applied, 'cockney' refers to a Londoner who was born 'within the sounds of the Bow-bells'. They were the bells of St Mary-le-Bow, the church situated in the very centre of the city. Like most of the buildings, they were destroyed in 1941 by German bombs, but like the sanctuary, have been restored since.

Much thought has been given to the origin of the nickname, first used in the seventeenth century. Many an explanation proffered is fictitious. This applies to the fanciful claim that it was the result of the cockneys' cheekiness. They were 'cocky' people. And for the cocky to become (a) cockney was not too far to go. It has equally been asserted that this designation grew out of country folks' contempt for the city dweller. Divorced from the soil, they had lost all contact with nature. They knew nothing about animals, crops and hard work. Pampered by the soft life, it could truly be said that they were *cockered*. A word now rarely used, it described anyone who was spoiled like a child. It may well have been suggested by the cockerel, kept and treated as a pet.

A seventeenth-century anecdote gives yet another reason

for the cockney's existence. It illustrates the disdain in which they were held at the time in the *Lexicon* published in 1617 by John Minshew, a 'Ductor in Linguas'. (An extraordinary work, it gives the equivalent of the words listed in eleven languages.) Accompanying his (derogatory) explanation of the cockney, Minshew relates an incident typical of the ignorance of city people.

He tells how 'a citizen's sonne riding with his father in the country, asked when he heard a horse neigh, what the horse did. His father answered, "Neigh". Riding further, he heard a cock crow and said "Does the *cock neigh*, too?" '. And that is how, according to Minshew, the cockney was born!

In reality, the cockney evolved from a 'cock's egg'. In medieval times this was known as *cokeney*. A malformed egg, it was the very first or last laid by a hen. Very small in size, it might even lack the yolk. Compared with a real egg, it was truly odd, without substance, just as the (London) cockney was a mere caricature of a real (country) person.

In their own inimitable way, the cockneys then changed the term intended to abuse and debase into a name of pride.

CODSWALLOP

The contents of a cod's stomach, it is said, made British naval personnel refer to worthless rubbish as codswallop. Therefore credit goes to those seamen to have added the word to English slang as a description of nonsense.

The 'wallop' part of the fish has meant different things at various times. Now obsolete, it once was used for 'gallop'. Subsequently, as it were, running away from its early beginnings, it took on the meaning of a thrashing. One of the (apocryphal) reasons given for the change once again is linked with the British navy and one of its successful actions in which it thoroughly defeated the French. The name of the admiral in charge of the attack was Wallop. In admiration, people came to say that he 'walloped' the French, making his name synonymous with a sound beating.

Ultimately, as late as the 1930s, wallop became an English colloquialism for 'beer'. Codswallop would come up in taste to its name—as undrinkable as a cod's brew.

COLD ENOUGH TO FREEZE THE BALLS OFF A BRASS MONKEY

To describe icy weather as 'cold enough to freeze the balls off a brass monkey' is not obscene, as some might imagine.

It is straight naval talk. 'Monkey' used to be the nickname for a young cadet, assigned with the duty to fetch the ammunition. His description was then transferred to the large brass plate on which the cannon balls were placed, accordingly called a brass monkey.

The practice created a problem. As the rate of contraction of the brass plate differed from that of the iron cannon balls, it so happened that in extremely cold weather the balls would roll off the much faster shrinking plate. Quite correctly, therefore, on such occasions the sailors could observe that it was 'cold enough to freeze the balls off a brass monkey'.

Another derivation has the same basic interpretation. However, it recognises in the 'brass monkey' a seventeenth-century sailors' nickname for the ship's cannon. When the temperature dropped far below freezing point, the iron balls, contracting at a different rate from the brass cannon, put it out of action!

Whichever way, the words were ambiguous. To avoid any misinterpretation, those anxious not to endanger their reputation slightly changed the saying, remarking that it was 'cold enough to freeze the ears off a brass monkey'.

COME A CROPPER

If someone fails completely, they 'come a cropper'. They do not fall on their feet but on their head, and 'crop' was an old description of it. The word comes from English riding slang, in which 'neck and crop' referred to the entire body of a horse. Someone who experienced total ruin is like a rider who tumbles off their mount head-over-heels, or a horse which falls to the ground.

Derived from a word for a swollen protuberance, in Old English (and still in the eighth century) 'crop' was specifically applied to the 'head' of herbs, shrubs and flowers. Farmers then used it for the 'heads' of vegetables they had planted and, as it was those alone they gathered at harvest time, they became known as their 'crop'.

Animals' preference to eat merely the succulent tops of grass made people say that they cropped it. In its multiple use and long history, crop, both as a noun and a verb, always ended up with the head—of the rider, the horse and the unlucky person whose misfortune, too, had come to a head, making them come a cropper.

COME TO A HEAD

For something to 'come to a head' is the climax of a development. The phrase has two interesting, but completely diverse explanations.

The expression has been traced to fifteenth-century England, when cabbage was the staple food. On maturing, the plant's leaves came together, making the vegetable look like a head. This is the reason why people still ask for 'a head of cabbage'.

Naturally, the process of ripening took time, and one can well imagine how anxious people were for the cabbage to mature, as well as their disappointment when being told by the grower that they would still have to wait for it 'to come to a head'.

Totally different is a derivation which links the phrase with boils and carbuncles. Before they could be lanced by the doctor, they had to 'come to a head'—meaning that the pus had to ripen.

COOL ONE'S HEELS

Anyone forced to wait cools their heels. This odd figure of speech originated at the time when the horse served as the principal means of transportation, either as a mount or in pulling a coach. When, on long trips, its hoofs became heated, the rider or driver had to stop and interrupt the journey to let them cool down. Though, as the saying goes, horses are (now only) for courses, in the manner of speaking, people still cool their heels when kept waiting.

COPPER

For policemen to be nicknamed 'coppers' may reflect the fact that one of their main duties was to 'cop' criminals. One hypothesis, in fact, traces the description to ancient Roman days in which a similar-sounding Latin word—*capere*—referred to the 'catching' of thieves.

A conspicuous feature on the London policeman's early uniform jacket was its shiny copper buttons. These caught people's eyes and ultimately were identified with the guardian of the law, who became 'the copper'. The nickname has stuck, though the original buttons have long been removed.

As in England police officers are often known as constables, it has also been suggested that the 'cop' is really an acronym, combining the first letters of a **c**onstable **o**n **p**atrol.

COTTON ON

Those who 'cotton on' quickly get the meaning of something explained to them. But this was not the original connotation of the phrase. Initially, those who 'cottoned on' had taken a fancy or a liking to a person or an idea. They clung to them. They did so just as bits of cotton did in eighteenth-century English weaving mills. Floating about, the fibres got stuck in the machinery or on the workers' hair and garments.

CRANKY

Anyone who is cranky owes the description of their bad-tempered condition to the same source responsible for the naming of the mechanical crank, the handle which is 'bent' or 'twisted'.

Though, to start with, chiefly an Americanism, applied to an eccentric person full of quirks and mentally 'twisted', no doubt *krank*, the German word for being 'sick' consolidated the term's meaning. After all, many Americans were of German stock and therefore well acquainted with the language.

The crank owed its final acceptance—in 1881—(as a word, not a person) to one man who gave it widest currency. He was Charles Guiteau, the assassin of President Garfield. On numerous occasions he used it, either for himself or for others. He did so in newspaper interviews he gave in prison and when speaking to the prosecutor during his trial. The subsequent reports, conspicuously featuring the 'crank', gave him his permanent place in its twisted sense.

CROWBAR

The association of the crowbar, that useful tool, with the bird is one of mere appearance. The grappling, wedge-shaped beak at one end reminded people of a crow's foot. This, as it were, got stuck in the tool for all time.

CROW'S NEST

Prior to modern navigation systems with their technology and electronic aids, sailors very much depended on their eyes to find their way across the wide expanses of the ocean. For this purpose, one of the sailors kept constant watch from a lookout. To have an unobstructed view, he took his place in a basket fixed at the highest possible point of the vessel, the very head of the mast. No wonder his perch reminded people of a bird's nest, and as the crow was well-known to them as the largest roosting bird, they called the lookout after it, a crow's nest.

Historically, it is thought that the earliest such observation post, in the form of a barrel, was used by whaling vessels. It enabled the whalers to discover from afar their prey, by the creatures' spouts. It also helped them in wintry seasons safely to traverse ice-bound stretches of water.

An alternate suggestion claims that the name of the crow's nest was based on a much more realistic former practice. Boats used to carry in a basket or cage a number of birds, including crows. If lost at sea and unable to find their way back to dry land, the crew released the birds who instinctively flew towards the land, thereby acting as invaluable guides.

CRYING OUT LOUD

The apparently innocuous exclamation of amazement or resentment, 'for crying out loud', like many other oaths, is a euphemism for something that once was regarded too blasphemous to be voiced in so many words. 'For crying out loud' was used instead of 'for Christ's sake' first in the United States in 1924. To avoid profaning Christ's name, it was camouflaged beyond recognition.

CURFEW

Curfews nowadays are imposed on towns, cities and districts to subdue or contain trouble. A military or police measure, it restricts people's movement in specified areas or at certain periods of time, mainly after dark. Those affected have to remain indoors.

The etymology of the term reveals its original use in totally different circumstances and far removed from tumultuous times.

From the French, curfew spoke of 'covering [up the] fire'—*couvre feu*. During the Middle Ages, when the majority of homes were built of timber or other easily combustible material, fire hazards were a constant threat. A single house on fire in no time could start a devastating conflagration, easily spreading through and destroying an entire village. It could be started by just one spark from an unattended open grate.

A wise precaution, therefore, was the enforcement of a regulation compelling every householder to cover up the fire in their grate during the night. This had to be done at a fixed time, publicly announced by the ringing of a bell which, accordingly, became known as the curfew bell. It served as a reminder to everyone and marked the birth of the modern curfew.

Cut and dried

Things arranged and finalised without a chance of change are said to be 'cut and dried'. The phrase originated in the processing of timber. Once cut and dried, it was ready for use.

Another suggestion, giving the words a completely different slant, links them with the practice of seventeenth-century herbalists. They sold their remedies not in the form of freshly-picked plants, but prepared for immediate consumption or application: cut and dried.

Deadline

To meet a 'deadline' is a somewhat gruesome description for the urgency of a task, oddly employed nowadays by authors, journalists and many others.

Originally, however, the phrase was not a mere metaphor, but very real. It goes back to the American Civil War and to Andersonville in Georgia (some 80 kilometres (50 miles) from Macon), the site of the notorious prisoner-of-war camp established by the Confederate forces.

It covered an area of less than 16 acres (6.6 ha) and lacked proper sanitation. At times, 30 000 men were jammed into the stockade—without sufficient food. Between February 1864 and its closure in April 1865 more than 45 000 members of the Union army were confined in it. Thirteen thousand captives perished from disease, overcrowding, exposure, malnutrition or other unidentified causes.

The agonies suffered generated enormous bitterness and anger. Captain Henry Wirz, its commandant, a Swiss mercenary, was described as a vicious sadist, a monster and a beast. At the abandonment of the camp, he was arrested and, once hostilities had ceased, was tried by a military court. Found guilty, he was executed for his war crimes. Later historians have attempted to exonerate him, attributing the horrible conditions of his camp to circumstances beyond his control.

The prison was surrounded by an almost impregnable palisade. Sentry boxes, nicknamed 'pigeon roosts', were positioned all along its top. It was said that they afforded the guards 'a comfortable place in which to stand and watch what was going on inside the camp'.

Parallel to the stockade, wooden stakes, driven into the ground at intervals formed an imaginary line, beyond which no prisoner was permitted to proceed. Whoever did so nevertheless, in an unsuccessful bid to make a run for freedom, was shot dead on sight. No wonder that the imaginary boundary became known as the deadline—the first in history.

DEUCE

Deuce, derived from the French *deux*, for 'two', has found its way into the scoring of tennis, the playing of cards and even into American criminal slang for a two-year prison sentence. Best-known, however, is its use as a mild expletive.

'Deuce' is the gamblers' exclamation at their lowest throw of dice, the 'two'. For them it is the most unfortunate number, spelling bad luck. This gave the figure altogether, mispronounced as 'deuce', an evil connotation, soon to be identified with the devil.

This came in handy for those too afraid to call the devil by his real name, and thus added yet another word to the long list of euphemisms used for him. It was a precautionary measure, based on the widespread belief that literally to speak of the devil was dangerous. Hearing his name, it would conjure him up and make him cause mischief. That is how 'What the deuce!' became a curse, blurted out not merely when unfortunate in playing dice but, generally, when frustrated or in anger.

There is also the assumption that in common speech 'deuce' came to take the place of the devil for the simple fact that the word shared with him and all things *d*amned, the initial.

The deuce of the outcry has been seen as well as all that is left of the name of a giant of ancient German myth and of a Celtic phantom figure.

One suggestion—going to the other extreme—recognises in the deuce of the exclamation not a call on the devil but on God. However, not to offend the divinity by the profane use of his name, people express it in this context in Latin as *deus* and, to camouflage it even further, changed the *deus* into deuce.

DIDDLE

The London stage has made many a lasting contribution to culture. It has even enriched the English vocabulary with all those who 'diddle'. The word used for petty swindling was adopted from the name of the chief character in a farce. Written by James Kenney, it was first performed in 1803.

A small-time crook, Jeremy Diddler, made his living by constantly obtaining small loans. He did so from every possible source and on any pretext—without ever repaying them. His method of raising finance gave Kenney the idea to call his farce *Raising the Wind*.

The play caught on, and with it, popularised Diddler's name and people described malpractices of his kind as 'diddling'. The new word gained even wider currency from an Edgar Allan Poe essay dedicated to Diddler's pursuit—'Diddling considered as One of the Exact Sciences'.

Most likely, Kenney created his character's name from 'duddle', a sixteenth-century dialect word used for cheating and tricking.

DIE WITH ONE'S BOOTS ON

'Dying with one's boots on', as a modern phrase, reflects heroism and determination. Whoever does so, has carried on to the very end. Dying in harness, one never retired or surrendered. That 'they died with their boots on' was the highest praise that could be given to soldiers. The saying gained popularity in an Errol Flynn movie based on General

George Custer's last stand with his 700 troops of the US Seventh Cavalry at the Battle of Little Bighorn. The film was entitled *They Died with Their Boots On*.

Initially though, the phrase—of American origin—had no laudatory connotation. Criminals, guilty of heinous crimes and condemned to die on the gallows, were hanged still wearing their boots! Unfortunately, so did the victims of violent death. Neither had the comfort to pass away peacefully in their beds.

DIFFERENT AS CHALK AND CHEESE

To underscore the unlikeness of two people, situations or substances, it is said that they are as different as chalk and cheese. To differentiate between chalk and cheese seems so easy. Not even the most ignorant could confuse the two. It is easy to imagine that their so obvious contrast was responsible for the analogy.

Nevertheless, there is much more to the original phrase. It recalls former fraudulent trade practices!

In the process of modern cheese making a colouring agent is used. It distinguishes the cheese not only in appearance but in taste. Centuries ago, however, cheese was 'naturally' white—as white as chalk. Tricksters took advantage of this similarity by selling to unsuspecting housewives pieces of suitably-shaped chalk, as cheese! This malpractice was responsible for the popular simile to stress the striking contrast.

DILDO

Suggestively, the artificial penis is said to have been named 'dildo' after the Italian *diletto*, meaning 'delight', which it promised to give to those using it.

DOCK

The enclosure occupied by the defendant in a court of law is known as the 'dock'. A strange choice of word, it is reminiscent of naval dockyards. However, there is no connection between the two.

The judicial dock can be traced to the Flemish tongue in which the word initially described a type of cage, particularly a pigsty, a chicken coop or a rabbit hutch. Charles Dickens popularised the word in its modern connotation which led to its general adoption. It shows the influence an author can have on his native tongue.

The nautical dock, on the other hand, goes back to the end of the fifteenth century, when (in 1495) the term was first applied to the Royal Dock at Portsmouth, England, and adopted from its earlier use for the groove a boat left in the mud or sand after having been beached for repairs or pulled up at high tide.

Though of such diverse backgrounds and, linguistically, of such different parentage, one having been born on the waterfront and the other coming out of a cage, both 'docks' share, after all, a common purpose. They secure or prevent from drifting or escaping whatever or whomever they hold.

DOG-EARED

Dog-eared pages are so called because the reader, lacking a proper book mark, has turned down the corner which thus looks much like a dog's ear, flopping over.

DOGHOUSE

Those in disgrace are said to be in the doghouse. It is a drastic way to show one's displeasure. Often applied to a wife punishing her husband for things done (or left undone), in no uncertain terms it tells her (not so) 'better half' that he is not fit to share her bed. His proper place is to sleep with the dog. To spend the night in a kennel is not exactly the most comfortable way for a human, particularly in inclement weather, not to mention the fleas...

In his famous story *Peter Pan*, Sir James Barrie tells how Nana, the Darling children's Newfoundland pet dog which served them as nursemaid as well, had been shabbily treated by their father. Realising how unkind he had been to the animal and feeling ashamed of it, in self-inflicted punishment he went to live in the doghouse! When the tale of *Peter Pan* captured people's imagination, it perpetuated the 'doghouse'.

There is the suggestion that gruesome reality rather than fiction was responsible for the idiom. It was linked with the African slave trade and the ships which carried their unhappy cargo across the Atlantic. During the night the victims were shackled in the holds. Afraid that they might break their chains and rebel, to ensure their own safety their guards and captors improvised sleeping places on deck, above the hatches covering the floating prison. To protect themselves against the cold and wind, they used small cubicles which, because of their uncomfortable constricted space, were soon nicknamed doghouses.

Dog in the manger

Whoever begrudges another's pleasure of something which is useless to himself, and stops them from enjoying it, is contemptuously called 'a dog in the manger'. This designation is based on yet another of Aesop's fables.

The fable tells of a dog who took up position near a manger full of hay. It did so viciously to prevent cattle and horses from getting near it. As the dog did not eat hay, it did not want others to enjoy it either.

Dot on the 'i'

A mere metaphor now, to be meticulous and exact, people are reminded to 'dot the i's (and cross the t's)'. Originally, however, the saying was taken very literally. The dot was added only later on, around the eleventh century, and for a pertinent reason.

In early calligraphy, two i's following each other in a text could easily be confused with the letter 'u'. To avoid such error, scribes felt the need to identify the letter so distinctly that it became unmistakable. For this purpose, they crowned it with a dot!

Etymologically, the dot itself has an intriguing past. Prior to topping the letter 'i', the dot referred to the head of a boil and a nipple.

Doughnuts

Doughnuts are so called because originally they were fried sweetened *dough*, in the shape of solid balls, called *nuts*.

Though now typically American, they were introduced by the Pilgrim Fathers who had acquired a liking for them during their stay in the Netherlands on their way to New England. They picked up the recipe, as it were, from the Dutch who, frying the dough in hogs' fat, referred to the pastry as 'oily cakes'.

The modern doughnut is ring-shaped. Wits suggest that the best recipe for making a doughnut was to take a hole and surround it with dough!

Hanson Crocket Gregory, a 15-year-old American youth, is credited with inventing it in 1847. He lived at Rockport in the state of Maine. Although he very much enjoyed eating his mother's fried round pastries, he had one complaint. While they were crisp on the outside, their centres were always soggy.

Speaking to his mother about it, she explained to him that she was well aware of it, but that it was not her fault. In fact, to overcome the problem, several times she had kept the cakes longer on the fire—with the result that they were burnt. Hanson accepted her answer, but did not take it as final. He felt that there had to be a solution and, ingeniously, he found it in the simplest possible way. Using a knife, he removed the centre of the round pastry before his mother fried it. This gave it the novel shape of a ring which was neither burnt nor soggy.

Making a hole in the story itself, as it were, is another version. This claims that Hanson Gregory was not a schoolboy, but a sea captain. He had invented the hole in the doughnut for a practical reason. He realised that a helmsman, whilst on duty for long periods then, must get hungry. He needed some refreshment, which a cake or bun could well provide. However, there was the problem of how to keep these within easy reach and ready for the eating without interfering with his task. It was so simple, Gregory found. By making a hole in the cakes, they could easily be slipped on the spokes of the wheel from which the helmsman could serve himself whenever he felt hungry and could do so without leaving his post.

There is even a tradition that an American Indian was responsible for the hole. Watching one of the Pilgrim women frying the traditional (Dutch) cakes, he shot an arrow through it. Too late to reshape the half-cooked doughnut and too poor to dispose of it, she finished frying it. The hole left at its centre made it all the more crisp and delicious. It caught people's fancy and made the hole a fixture in all the doughnuts cooked since.

DRACONIAN

To speak of anything as Draconian emphasises its harshness. It is one of the many expressions called after an historic figure.

Draco was an Athenian legislator and the first to codify the laws of Athens (in 621 BC). The penalties he introduced were most severe. Draco showed little pity even for the most minor offences. Relieving oneself in public was thus regarded a grievous misdemeanour and accordingly punished. Creditors were entitled to enslave a debtor who was unable to repay the money owed. On the mere suspicion of having committed manslaughter while abroad, a traveller was refused re-entry into the country until he had been cleared of the charges. In fact, the majority of crimes (which included the stealing of a head of cabbage) carried the death sentence.

No wonder that, traditionally, it was said that Draco had written his laws in blood—both metaphorically and literally. His name became synonymous with the merciless and ruthless execution of justice.

When challenged about why he had made his penalties so savage, he replied that it was his opinion that small offences merited death, while he could think of no harsher penalty for greater crimes.

Nevertheless, to regard 'Draconian law' merely as something negative is unfair. It ignores Draco's significant place in legal history. He has the credit to have been the first in Greece to abolish the practice of taking personal revenge, and to replace it with a strictly controlled system of objective justice, at least as it was understood in his day.

His legislation was not to last for long. Within 27 years, Solon, one of the 'seven sages' of Greece, repealed Draco's entire code, with only one exception, the law dealing with homicide. In spite of it, 'draconian' as a description of anything 'cruel' and 'severe' has survived to the present day.

DRAW THE LINE

People may tolerate certain behaviour and permit things to happen—up to a point. But then they refuse to go any further. That is when they 'draw the line'.

At first thought, it might be imagined that the line employed in the figure of speech referred to a rope stretched across to stop anyone from going beyond it. However, the phrase, taken very literally, might speak of a geometrical line. Drawn on the ground, it indicated a limit in a game, a sport or a fight. Opinions differ as from which of these the phrase was first derived.

Chief contender is tennis. A line drawn on either side of the improvised court indicated how far the ball could be hit before it was 'out'. Boxing also has been cited. A line scratched in the sand of the boxing ring showed the limit to which a contestant could advance.

Totally different is yet a third suggestion. It traces this idiomatic line to medieval peasants' fields. Cut by ploughshares, it clearly designated the boundary of their property, beyond which they were not allowed to harvest.

DRESSED (UP) TO THE NINES

Anyone clothed very elegantly is colloquially 'dressed (up) to the nines'. The choice of the number has been related to the significant part it has played in mythology, mysticism and reckoning. In the traditional scale of values, rising from one to ten, nine was closest to perfection. Hence, those dressed up to the nines had almost reached it.

In classical times, it was believed that the world of art, literature and science was controlled by the nine muses. Their number represented the total sum of everything that attracted and inspired the mind, just as would a person conspicuous by the smartness of dress.

Nine was three times three, the figure Pythagoras had already regarded as 'the perfect number'. Therefore it trebled its supreme value.

Ninepins once was a popular pastime. Those spending an evening out playing the game were said to have gone 'to the nines'. Properly dressed for the occasion, they were 'dressed (up) to the nines'.

Many of these explanations, obviously, are far-fetched. No wonder doubts have been raised regarding the use of the nine altogether and it is thought that it might not be part of the phrase in any figurative sense at all. What now appears as a 'nine' is the remnant of an Old English word, misunderstood and, subsequently, wrongly divided.

People exquisitely attired were said to be dressed 'up to the eyes'. Their smartness extended all over, from the feet up to their very eyes. 'To the eyes' in Old English was *to then eyne*. When grammar and words changed, it was no longer realised that *eyne* was the plural of an eye. This led people to make the wrong connection, linking the final 'n' of the preceding and by then obsolete article 'the*n*' to the archaic eyes, in 'the nines'.

Dressing down

To put someone in their place by giving them a 'dressing down' has nothing to do with clothes. It might merely perpetuate the once common use of the word 'dressing' for the 'scolding' of a person, setting them right. Equally possible is the crossover of the term from the meat trade. A butcher is said to 'dress down' a carcass when cutting it up. And whoever is being given a severe reprimand (a 'dressing down'), metaphorically, is cut into pieces.

Probably though, the figure of speech is not a survival of outdated English nor borrowed from butchers' terminology, but comes from the early mining of ore. When rock containing the metal had been dug out of the ground, prior to being crushed in the mill or going to the smelter, it was broken up into small pieces, a process termed 'dressing down'. Anyone being severely told off must have felt crushed or broken up— as were those pieces.

Drop a clanger

A clang is a resounding noise, like that made by a struck bell. To 'drop a clanger' is to say something so embarrassing or to blunder so badly that it cannot go unnoticed. As it were, it reverberates in people's mind like—in modern parlance—a sonic boom.

Dyed in the wool

A dyed-in-the-wool member of a party or association is thoroughly imbued with its ideas. Their opinions are so deep-seated and have become so much part of them, that nothing can change them.

Cloth woven out of wool which has been dyed before is colourfast. It is 'dyed in the wool' and can be washed without the colour bleeding. This makes it very different from cloth dyed only after it has been woven.

EARRINGS
EAT ONE'S WORDS
EATING THE AMERICAN WAY
EVERY DOG HAS ITS DAY

EARRINGS

Originally earrings were exactly what they are called—plain rings. They were worn both by men and women, and for several reasons.

Haunted by the belief that malevolent forces were constantly surrounding them, people had to protect themselves. What better means was there than to use the magic circle in the form of the ring. Symbolic of the (round) sun, it would drive away the servants of the world of darkness. These were further intimidated by the ring being a shiny object, reflecting light. The ring thus became a powerful charm twice over.

So that it would not be lost, the ring was firmly attached to some part of the body, one of the lips, the nose or, not least, the ears, for which purpose the lobes were pierced. The choice of the ears had other weighty motives, also going back to early superstitions. Members of many varied races took particular care to guard all the orifices of their body because it was through them, they believed, that evil spirits could easily enter and possess them. Though it was possible to close one's eyes, one could not close one's ears which, therefore, were most vulnerable and needed safeguarding.

In their many hostile encounters, native tribes had difficulty in differentiating between friend and foe. Without uniforms and only wearing a loincloth, they had no specific means of identification. This was yet another reason for the wearing of earrings. The objects used, of varied material and colour, served as a means of recognition. Unlike the modern identity card, the rings never wore out nor could be hidden away. Conspicuously, they stuck out.

Other potent and useful faculties were attributed to the rings. They were thought to ward off disease and to have curative powers. In more modern days, they were worn as well to serve as a highly valued reminder. Sailors, especially prone to superstition because of the vagaries of the sea, not only believed in the efficacy of the earring as a charm, but that the piercing of their lobes would improve their eyesight. This enabled them to see further at sea, which added to their safety, particularly so prior to the introduction of the telescope.

It was a British custom for a sailor's wife to present her husband with one of her earrings whenever he went to sea. Carefully, she retained the other. She did so not merely superstitiously, for good luck, but magically to ensure his safe return. Not least, it was also to remind him of her constant love, however far and long he was away at sea.

Far from being just an ornament and a piece of jewellery, the earring has thus played a significant role in humankind's perpetual struggle for survival and striving for security and happiness, and reflects the deep-rooted conviction that it could affect the wearer's health and fortune.

EAT ONE'S WORDS

Of those who have to retract an opinion and admit that what they had previously stated was wrong, it is said that they have 'to eat their words'.

The gastronomical figure of speech stems from the Bible, but is used there in a totally different sense. At a moment of depression caused by the apparent failure of his mission, the prophet Jeremiah recalled the days when he had joyfully welcomed God's message. Just as one has pleasure in eating something tasty, so—metaphorically speaking—did he then eat the divine words (Jer. 15:16).

A second and even more explicit source of the phrase is a passage in the writings of the prophet Ezekiel. It tells (Ez. 3:1–2) how he was asked by God to eat a scroll, inscribed with divine words of lamentations, mourning and woe, addressed to the people. Carrying the symbolism further, he was urged to devour the entire contents of the scroll and, in spite of its ominous meaning, to do so as eagerly as a famished man would eat a meal.

The Bible continues to relate how Ezekiel ate the awesome words which were in his mouth 'as honey for sweetness'. Authorities have tried to explain such extraordinary paradox. For a servant of God it was 'sweet' to be privileged to execute the divine will and to be entrusted by the Almighty with any task, no matter what it was.

To 'eat one's words' was so striking a figure of speech that it stuck in the mind. However, the circumstances and context were forgotten. Totally divorced from the biblical source, it acquired the almost opposite meaning of recanting, the taking back of something one had said.

EATING THE AMERICAN WAY

Americans particularly appreciate the value of time. Masters in the study of time and motion, they have learnt to streamline life in many ways. Incongruously though, they waste time whenever they sit down for a meal. Conspicuous to outsiders, they then follow a peculiar custom. First, they cut up the meat—holding the fork in their left hand and the knife in their right. They then put down the knife and change the fork over to their right hand to pick up the individual pieces and the vegetables. An involved procedure, it makes Americans 'stand out' in any crowd.

The origin of the American way of eating shows how traditions of the past are perpetuated, even if their once useful reason no longer holds true.

In the early pioneering days, knives were in short supply and it often happened that a family possessed only one knife. It was therefore only natural that, when sitting down for a meal, the head of the house was privileged to use the knife first. After having cut up his food, he passed the knife on to the next member of the family who, in turn, after having used it, handed it on. With the knife thus making the round, each individual had only a fork left. Obviously, this was now held in the right hand. The habit became so ingrained that even when knives became plentiful, the early mode of eating was never abandoned.

EVERY DOG HAS ITS DAY

History has shown that even those most discriminated against and maltreated have reason to hope. The time will come (however far distant and shortlived) when they will gain recognition and, at least for one day, fortune will smile on them.

Proverbially, their fate has been compared with that of a canine: 'every dog has its day'. Though it is not known who coined the metaphor, the first mention can be traced back to 1545. Fifty-five years later, Shakespeare made Hamlet say: 'The cat will mew and dog will have his day'. Making the observation more embracing, Carlyle added (in 1837) that it applied even to rabid dogs.

No doubt, of all creatures dogs have had the most miserable past. In some parts of the world they were true outcasts. Considered unclean, they were kicked and chased away. Harassed all their life, nonetheless, the moment came when they could show their mettle and prevail for at least a short while.

FALL GUY

FENCE

FIASCO

FIGHT LIKE KILKENNY CATS

FIGHTING FIRE WITH FIRE

FINK

FISHY BUSINESS

FLASH IN THE PAN

FLAT SPIN

FLEA MARKET

FLY OFF THE HANDLE

FOOT THE BILL

FOUR-POSTER BED

FRENCH PASTRY

FRESH AS A DAISY

FROG IN THE THROAT

FROM THE FRYING PAN INTO THE FIRE

FUDDY-DUDDY

FURPHY

FUZZ

Fall guy

Sport but not sportsmanship has created the fall guy. He started in wrestling. However, he did so during a period (in the nineteenth century) when contests had sadly deteriorated into mere shows—with their outcome 'fixed' in advance!

The fall guy's name literally described his role. For the aggrandisement of his opponent, the preselected champion, he was the *guy* who had to *fall* to the ground and to do so most convincingly. It was all arranged and rigged, and he was paid for the performance, which it really was. What at first was mere play-acting changed into a much less enjoyable job. His adversary in the sham encounter began to enjoy knocking him down and to treat him ruthlessly.

That is how, eventually, from pure showmanship and the wrestling stage the fall guy entered everyday life to become the description of any loser and dupe, particularly of people who are the victims of confidence tricksters or who are given the blame for things they have never done and crimes they have not committed.

Fence

In criminal terminology and slang, whoever trades in stolen property is a fence. This name was well-chosen. It alluded to the precaution of keeping certain activities under cover and goods bought and sold hidden away—'fenced off'. To be known as a fence recalls their 'de*fence*' against discovery. The fence, then, has surrounded themselves with a special guard. Of equal linguistic derivation is the fender which, when attached to a car or a railway engine thrusts away any obstruction, and when placed in front of a fireplace, prevents any of its contents from spilling on to the floor and, when alight, possibly setting the house on fire.

They all have a common Latin root—*fendere*, shared by any

type of defence and the sport of fencing as well, which the modern fence has misappropriated.

FIASCO

The origin of the fiasco is the Italians' description of a failure as 'making a bottle'. Not a mere figure of speech, it is based on what is claimed to have been a practice of Venetian glass-blowers. It sometimes happened that in the process of making one of their beautiful creations, things went wrong and the intended intricate design was spoiled. Not to waste the precious glass, they made it into a bottle—*fiasco* in Italian.

Also Italian in origin, but belonging to the stage, is another derivation of this internationally-recognised designation of a flop in the form of a flask. It tells how a comedian, unable to raise a laugh, loudly blamed the failure on the flask (*fiasco*) which was part of the (misfired) performance.

The Italian fiasco, it has been pointed out, was not an ordinary sort of bottle. Long-necked, it had a rounded base and therefore, unless specially provided with a support, could not stand upright on its own. A fiasco, according to this interpretation, suggested an effort or enterprise undertaken lacking an essential feature, which made it collapse.

FIGHT LIKE KILKENNY CATS

The Irish town of Kilkenny has a colourful past with a rich history. It has become world-famous through its cats. 'To fight like Kilkenny cats' means to battle ferociously to the bitter end.

Until 1844, the city was divided into two parts, segregating the native Irish from the Anglo-Normans. Constantly at loggerheads, they often came to blows. They fought like cats, people said. The observation survived the struggle but, forgetting its merely metaphorical sense, it was misinterpreted. Imagining that it referred particularly to the town's felines, these were misrepresented as being exceptionally belligerent.

Gruesome are two other traditions. Each of them traces the phrase to a specific incident in the city's history.

Hessian soldiers who had served as mercenaries in the British army against the Americans were billeted for some time on their way home in County Kilkenny. After all the excitement of battle, they soon were bored. To pass away the time and amuse themselves, they caught stray cats. After tying their tails together, they threw them across a clothes line, and watched the unfortunate creatures struggle to get down.

Hearing their yowling, the commanding officer rushed from his quarters to investigate the cause of the rumpus. Afraid of disciplinary action for their cruel pastime, the men quickly tried to cover it up. They freed the cats by cutting off their tails with a sword. The poor animals ran away as fast as they could. There was no time left, however, for the soldiers to remove the knotted tails from the line. On being questioned about them, they explained that the Kilkenny cats, renowned fighters, had engaged once again in so fierce a battle that all that was left of them were their tails!

(A slightly different version relates the occurrence to the occupation of the town by Cromwell and his rampaging troops.)

Another derivation of the saying links it with sportsmen. They had heard a rumour that Kilkenny cats excelled all others in fighting prowess. To verify the story, they caught 1000 'ordinary' cats from all the other counties, to pit them against 1000 Kilkenny felines. The latter lived up to their reputation. In no time they confronted the intruders, attacking them viciously. The battle raged all night. At sunrise, all that remained of the 1000 intruders were their badly-mauled bodies. The 1000 Kilkenny cats had survived the fight. Though looking the worse for it, their fighting spirit was undiminished. 'To fight like Kilkenny cats' is thus the remnant of the unsportsmanlike sporting event.

Without reducing their fighting quality, a popular verse limits it to two cats:

> There once were two cats in Kilkenny,
> Each thought there was one cat too many,
> So they fought and they fit
> And they scratched and they bit
> Until instead of two cats there weren't any.

FIGHTING FIRE WITH FIRE

'Fighting fire with fire' is both an effective practice to confine a blaze, and a figure of speech for a drastic response to an act of aggression.

In some regions, during the heat of summer, forest and bush fires are a constant threat. They can engulf entire woods or tracts of land and burn homes built in clearings.

To extinguish or even merely to contain such conflagrations is a very difficult task. At times, the only option left is to burn firebreaks, literally therefore 'fighting fire with fire'. An emergency measure thus taken in a desperate situation was responsible for the saying.

It is often the case that to overcome a threat, kind words and mild actions prove insufficient. The menace has to be met by measures of equal strength, magnitude, and, if need be, identical but regrettable tactics. This, too, is the meaning of 'fighting fire with fire' and an alternate source of the metaphor.

FINK

'Fink' is an exclusively American term, born in the country's labour movement. It was first used to brand those who harmed the cause of working people in their fight for their rights and better labour conditions.

This unsubtle put-down has been associated with the famous Pinkerton National Detective Agency, because of the part some of its officers took in helping employers against their employees. They used every possible means to break up strikes. They acted as informers or spies, posing as workers to report on the clandestine activities of union members. Most notorious was the unsuccessful attempt in 1892 of 300 of its detectives—who were armed—to stop the industrial action taken by the workers of the Carnegie Steel Company in Homestead, Pennsylvania.

No wonder that labourers all over the country soon transferred their hatred to all the Pinkerton men and, in their mind, the name of the agency became synonymous with acts of infamy. Contemptuously, they cut down its name to Pink which they then further changed to fink, as the derogatory designation for a strikebreaker and a stool pigeon.

It is a somewhat involved derivation and therefore gives greater credibility to other suggestions, not necessitating any change of name!

One such claim quotes Albert Fink as the 'original' fink. German-born (in 1827), he migrated to the United States in 1849. Working for the railroads, eventually he was put in charge of its team of detectives. In pursuit of his duties, he incurred the wrath of the men, who decried him as a squealer and a police informer. This made his name a byword, synonymous with those who degrade themselves by ignominiously interfering with the lives of other people.

There is yet another theory. As many Americans came from Germany, they might well have brought with them the 'fink' as a typical name of contempt. It was used in their native land, specifically in the academic world. Undergraduates were expected to join students' associations. Highly organised, these demanded of their members to adhere to a strict code of behaviour at all times. They were to show discipline and to wear with pride the colours of their particular 'union'.

There were students, however, of independent minds. They preferred to do things their own way and refused to abide by the unions' inhibiting rules and regulations. They much rather followed a permissive lifestyle, of lax and loose morals. Naturally, the unions looked askance at them and showed their displeasure by calling any such outsider a *Fink* (first in Jena in c. 1740). At the time, this was a popular name given to people of lowest standing and ill-repute. Its choice goes back to nature. A finch was called in German a *Fink*. The bird was notorious for its obnoxious custom of picking its feed out of horses' manure. To be called after a creature of such dirty habits was regarded as just the right thing for those whose behaviour seemed to ask for it.

FISHY BUSINESS

Fish are slippery and therefore difficult to hold in one's hand. No wonder that this experience created all 'fishy business', in the way of speaking. A fishy customer cannot be trusted.

FLASH IN THE PAN

It often happens that innovations, enterprises and novel ideas lauded as revolutionary and likely to change an entire way of life soon come to naught and are forgotten altogether. Anything thus showing much promise but disappointingly petering out in no time has been compared to a 'flash in the pan'.

The figure of speech does not come from the frying pan in the kitchen but from the battlefield. It goes back to the days of weaponry when the charge of a flintlock gun was fired by igniting powder in its pan. This was done by means of a spark produced by pulling the trigger which made a steel hammer strike a flint.

At times, it failed to set off the desired explosion. All it achieved was a momentary flash in the pan. Possibly the powder had not been kept dry enough or the gun was not properly cleaned.

Though the flint gun has been discarded long ago and now is only seen in museums, its abortive flash still lingers on, permanently to serve as an (outdated) metaphor for fleeting fame and shortlived success.

FLAT SPIN

A common situation in a society of ruthless competition, in which work under pressure has become part of the lifestyle, is to be in a 'flat spin'.

The expression, generally figuratively for a state of confusion, dates back to the 1920s when it described an actual phenomenon experienced in the early history of aviation. It was linked with the test flights of new-model aeroplanes.

To prove the airworthiness of a machine, the pilot made it go into a spiralling descent. If the pilot lost control, the nose of the plane would lift up and start to spin 'flatly'. It was a perilous manoeuvre because, if the pilot couldn't bring the craft out of the spin, it was bound to crash.

FLEA MARKET

It is generally claimed that the first flea market was held in Paris. The choice of its name (the French *marché aux puces*) was well founded. Offering a multitude of the most varied kinds of second-hand goods, not surprisingly many of the items were infested with fleas.

Improved hygiene and the use of modern insecticides have removed the fleas from the merchandise, but not from the name of the market, now adopted worldwide.

A most credible explanation, it has nevertheless been disputed. The credit, it is said, should go to the Americans, of Dutch colonial days. They were the real creators of the modern flea market, by many years preceding the French! More so, proudly they could also claim that their 'original' flea market was not named because of any vermin found in the wares sold. The name was the result of a mistake and—literally—a misunderstanding.

The open-air market was held in present-day New York City, then still the Dutch New Amsterdam. Its site was at the foot of Maiden Lane in Manhattan, popularly known as 'the valley'. It was only natural that people came to refer to it by its location as the 'valley' (or vallie) market, a name they soon shortened into (the Dutch-sounding) 'vlie' market. As in Dutch the 'v' is pronounced as 'f'. Anglicised this was rendered as the fly market or, most frequently, the flea market—without flies or fleas ever having played a role or plagued its customers!

FLY OFF THE HANDLE

Those flying off the handle by losing their temper can cause more than unpleasantness, they become a threat. They create as dangerous a situation as when an axe head flies off its handle. This was often the case in the 1800s, the very time American pioneers first used the phrase in its modern sense. It was based on their own experience. Axe handles then were improvised and crudely made. They could suddenly get detached and the axe, flying off, could hit anyone nearby, causing serious injury.

FOOT THE BILL

It was the custom for anyone presented with a bill not to settle it on the spot, but rather sign their name below the totalled-up amount—at its 'foot'. This signature was their promise to pay the account in due course. Its specific placement thus created the phrase 'to foot the bill', and eventually expanded to the settlement of any debt.

FOUR-POSTER BED

The four-poster bed with thick curtains enclosing it for many centuries had very practical reasons. An imposing piece of furniture, it was not merely a status symbol, but solved several problems. It originated at a time when hallways were non-existent and, failing a separate access to the various rooms, everyone had to pass through the bedroom. To ensure privacy for the occupant(s) of the bed, its curtains were drawn.

The four-poster had another advantage. In the northern winter, at a time when homes were badly insulated against the freezing air outside and poorly heated by open fires, it protected the sleepers against the cold and kept them warm.

FRENCH PASTRY

Surprisingly, on occasions carelessness and lack of attention have enriched the world and added to its pleasures. Our culinary delights thus owe something to the negligence of an unknown French pastry cook!

Preparing a short pastry, a French cook forgot to put butter into the dough. Becoming aware of his omission, he cut butter into small pieces, placing them on top of the rolled out mixture, which he then folded, rolled out again and refolded. Repeating the process several times, he was sure that the butter had thoroughly blended with the dough. This he then baked.

When removing the pastry from the oven, he discovered that it had turned flaky. It was the birth of French pastry!

FRESH AS A DAISY

Daisy is the contracted form of the Saxons' designation of the flower as the 'day's eye'. It was a beautiful and apt choice of name for so common a field plant. It revealed how observant and imaginative this early race was.

No doubt the Saxons were fascinated by the golden disk at the centre of the flower, so much like a glowing sun, and the petals radiating from it, like wide shiny rays. They equally took note how at sunset the flower closed its petals over its yellow centre, its 'eye', to unfold them again at dawn, as if it were reopening the eye. To their mind the flower then appeared re*fresh*ed after what seemed its night's sleep. This made them describe someone who had enjoyed a good rest as feeling 'as fresh as a daisy'.

FROG IN THE THROAT

Those speaking with a croaking voice are said to have a frog in the throat. Though, apparently, an appropriate and innocuous figure of speech, its origin might not be so harmless...

Its most common explanation recalls the days when, to quench their thirst, people drank from the nearest pond or well. In the process, they could easily swallow a frog or its spawn and it was truly believed that such an unfortunate occurrence accounted for the loss of voice. Gruesomely, it was further imagined that the frog in the throat had eventually moved down into the victim's stomach and was slowly devouring its host!

The expression might also be derived from a practice of medieval folk medicine. Its prescribed cure for what is now diagnosed as a throat infection or thrush in the throat was the application of a live frog. The patient was asked, without eating or swallowing it, to keep it inside the mouth, where the frog was thought to extract and, with its breath, exhale the disease from the human throat. Its healing function could be compared to an exhaust pipe!

The treatment has long been abandoned and people have learnt to drink only water that is unpolluted. Nevertheless, the 'frog in the throat' survives in everyday speech, whenever people refer to a croaky voice.

FROM THE FRYING PAN INTO THE FIRE

Those who try to extricate themselves from a predicament may aggravate matters instead of actually improving things. This is said to be jumping 'from the frying pan into the fire'. The metaphor could easily be assumed to reflect some unfortunate incident in the kitchen. In reality, it is borrowed from a heated religious controversy between two notable churchmen—William Tyndale and Sir Thomas More. Tyndale is renowned as the translator of the Bible into English and More as the author of *Utopia*, the famous portrayal of an ideal community, whose title, in fact, he contributed to the languages of the world.

More strongly disagreed with Tyndale's views, which he bitterly attacked in a treatise usually quoted as A *Dialoge Concerning Heresyes*. Tyndale, not lost for words, responded three years later in *An Answere unto Syr Thomas More's Dyaloge*. This did not silence More. Within two years, he wrote *The Confutacyon* [*Confutation*] *of Tyndale's Answere*.

It was in this literary ding-dong battle, that in 1528 More introduced the vivid metaphor into the English language. He applied it to Tyndale's abortive attempt to maintain and confirm his originally expressed opinion. More asserted that Tyndale, in fact, instead of strengthening his argument, had only further invalidated it. It was 'like a flounder which leaped out of a frying pan into the fire'. No doubt, he adopted the words from Tertullian, the second-century African church father and first Christian theologian to write in Latin, who had used the simile, without the flounder, in that ancient tongue.

FUDDY-DUDDY

A 'fuddy-duddy' is an unbending, old-fashioned 'stick-in-the-mud', particularly an elderly person with fixed ideas.

At first thought, this description may suggest an old *daddy*, muddled—be*fudd*led—by drink. As a fuddy-duddy, this person may represent another, linguistic, kind of blend: a fussy sort of fogey. The name may also be remindful of a dud. Like a shell that does not explode, it proves totally ineffective. To stress this person's utter uselessness this type of human dud is presented doubled-up—reduplicated, as a fuddy-duddy.

Unreal but amusing is an anecdote which tells how an American congregation created the fuddy-duddy—synthetically. Its minister was a very staid and narrow-minded clergyman. On the other hand, he was highly educated, with doctoral degrees both in philosophy and divinity. Proudly, he displayed these in their traditional abbreviation of PhD and DD behind his name. It did not take his parishioners long to give those characters a new meaning which, they felt, was most appropriate in his case. They stood, they said, for Phuddy-duddy.

FURPHY

Furphy, an Australianism for an unfounded rumour, originated in army camps during the First World War. From there it made its way into popular speech.

Furphy was the name of a Victorian foundry, called after John Furphy who had established it in Shepparton in 1874. It manufactured the carts used to supply water and the sanitary trucks used to remove sewage. These carts and trucks were seen daily in Victorian military camps, with the firm's name conspicuously displayed on them. Soon they became a popular meeting place for the men. Standing around them, they exchanged the latest gossip. In no time, 'Furphy' became synonymous with the (often latrine) rumours they spread, not least because of the contents of some of the vehicles.

Fuzz

Fuzz is one of the many and not always complimentary names given to the police. It was early cockney slang for anyone who was resented or disliked. How Londoners came to use it first in this sense has been given a variety of explanations.

Some believe that generally it reflected their contempt for those who were fussing (or fuzzing) around in matters that were really not their concern. Surely, no one did so more than a 'copper'. Overparticular in his demands and hard to please, he well deserved to be called a 'fuzz'.

On the other hand, fuzz might be all that remained from a hostile encounter of the British with Sudanese tribesmen. In Kipling's words, those 'pore benighted 'eathen' fighting men were given the nickname of fuzzy-wuzzies because of their curly hair. Shortened to 'fuzzy', it became the description of anyone to be avoided, as a policeman was by criminals.

Others have claimed that fuzz was an American term, though of doubtful origin. It has been seen as a corrupted version of 'feds', the nickname given to the *fed*eral narcotic agents by those engaged in early drug traffic. For reasons unknown, they transferred the description to policemen. Also American is yet another derivation. Over-zealous policemen who were hard to please were referred to as 'fussytails'. And it did not take long to change the fussytail into a fuzz.

G

GAY

GAZEBO

GET ONE'S GOAT

GET SOMETHING OFF ONE'S CHEST OR
TO MAKE A CLEAN BREAST

GET UNDER ONE'S SKIN

GOBBLEDEGOOK

GO IN ONE EAR AND OUT OF THE OTHER

GOING FOR A SONG

GOING GAGA

GONDOLA

GONE TO THE DOGS

GOOD FOOTING

GRAPEVINE

GREEN FINGERS AND A GREEN THUMB

GROOVY

GUNG HO

GAY

The term 'gay' has an intriguing story in the way it was once used and ultimately became the generally accepted term for homosexual. It has covered a long distance between its early connotation of a carefree person with a happy disposition to its present-day sexual application. At one time, it served even as a description of religious significance. In the 1680s in the American colonies, Quakers and the Pennsylvanian Dutch, while describing themselves as 'the plain people', referred to the more worldly-minded Lutherans as 'gay'.

It was only in Victorian times that the word became associated with sex. To be gay then meant to take liberties, and people so called were either living promiscuously or engaged in prostitution. A 'gay house' was a common name for a brothel, and people amorously inclined used to say that they 'felt gay'.

In its specific homosexual meaning, it is claimed, gay was first publicly mentioned in London in 1889, in the so called 'Cleveland Street scandal'. This concerned a homosexual brothel in the West End of the city, frequented by men in high office and serviced by post office boys.

When cross-examined by the police, John Saul, a male prostitute working in the house, described himself and his associates as 'gays', in the modern sense.

From Britain, the 'gay', in its new connotation, crossed the Atlantic to become an American euphemism for homosexuals, eventually to be proudly adopted by the Gay Liberation Movement.

Though there is an opinion that Australian slang used 'gay boy' for homosexuals already in the mid-1920s, generally the term gay in its new meaning took some time to be adopted 'down under'. This caused considerable embarrassment on President Johnson's visit to Sydney. Large banners suspended across the streets along which his motorcade was to proceed, welcomed him with the words, 'Let's Go Gay with LBJ'!

When the American advance party arrived and saw those banners, they were horrified. They pointed out the diplomatic implications of the Australian linguistic backwardness. As it was too late to remove the offending banners, American TV cameras televising the President's procession along the route to the 'folks back home' not accidentally always went out of focus when showing the gay banners.

Gazebo

A gazebo is a pavilion or some kind of lookout placed in an elevated position, to give people the opportunity to *gaze* out on the surrounding countryside. Gazebo thus really meant a 'gaze-about'.

Another suggestion asserts that it was not the actual 'gaze' that gave the structure its unusual name. This was artificially created by using the mock Latin *videbo* for 'I shall see'. Obviously, it referred to the spectacular view obtained from its windows.

Get one's goat

To get one's goat is irritating, especially if the goat is not really a goat but a beard. At one time it was fashionable for men to grow hair on their chin in a tuft-like outcrop. As it reminded people of a billygoat's beard, they called it a goatee. To have one's goat(ee) pulled was aggravating and annoying.

The phrase has also been linked with horse racing . A racehorse was often highly strung and hard to manage when kept in a stall on its own. It seemed to need company. To have it share its quarters with a second horse, however, did not work. To have another stallion as a companion only challenged and upset the racer all the more. A mare, on the other hand, was even less advisable. It could sexually excite the stallion and often at the most unsuitable moment.

It was discovered that, of all animals, a goat proved an ideal mate. Somehow, its presence calmed down the horse, particularly important prior to a race.

Well aware of this fact, dishonest rivals used to sneak into the stable during the night preceding the race to 'get the goat'. Having lost its stablemate, the horse became unsettled and agitated and could not win its race. And that is how 'to get one's goat', it was said, became synonymous with causing annoyance and irritation.

Originally, there was no goat at all in the phrase, is yet another suggestion. It found its way there merely by mistake and by people not properly enunciating words. The idiom referred to a goad, the sharp instrument once used to prod animals. The spur got stuck in people's slovenly speech, thus changing goad into goat.

Get something off one's chest or to make a clean breast

There is a valid reason, though buried in the past, for describing persons who confess a guilt or express a feeling or secret they had so far kept to themselves, as 'making a clean breast of it' or 'getting it off their chest'.

These go back to the time when offenders' chests were branded with the initial of the crime or sin they had committed. For adulterers to get the 'A' off their chests, for instance, was something greatly desired. Those guilty of an offence were factually described as having a 'stained breast'. To admit their failings and rid themselves of the burden that lay heavily on their conscience therefore, very appropriately, was referred to as 'making a clean breast'.

Get under one's skin

To get under one's skin, metaphorically, recalls an actual unpleasant physical experience of the past. Noxious insects and certain species of worms used to deposit their larvae under a person's skin. In the process of developing, they caused painful discomfort to their unwilling host.

More common still was the aggravating sensation felt by people who were stung by nettles. Subsequently they were irritated by the barbs which remained sticking under the skin!

Gobbledegook

Gobbledegook has been defined as pretentious, involved, verbose and incomprehensible jargon. A mere fog of words. It is used by people and government departments to be looked upon with awe and deference or as euphemisms and evasions, intended to blur unpleasant and damaging facts.

An American congressman, the Texan Maury Maverick (1895–1954), claimed to have invented the word. Attending a committee meeting of the Smaller War Plant Corporation, held in 1944 (during the Second World War), he had been aggravated by some of its members' pomposity. This was the case not least, when the chairman had spoken at length of 'maladjustments co-extensive with problem areas...alternative but nevertheless meaningful minimae' and the 'utilisation of factors which in a dynamic democracy can be channelised into both quantitive and qualitive phases'.

Giving vent to his feelings, Maverick subsequently sent out a memo castigating the practice of such unintelligible, obnoxious verbosity. He wrote, 'When concrete nouns are replaced by abstractions, simple terms by pseudo-technical jargon, the result is gobbledegook.'

He further gave instructions that henceforth such

'gobbledegook should be avoided at all costs'. He requested, 'Be short and say what you're talking about.'

Maverick was not certain how he came to choose the new word. In fact, at one time he felt that it must have come to him in a vision. On the other hand, much more down to earth, he explained to the *New York Times Magazine* on 21 May 1944 that he might have been thinking of the old bearded turkey gobbler back home in Texas. Strutting with ludicrous pomposity, this had always been gobbledy-gobbling and at the end of this gobble being a sort of gook—muck.

Disregarding Maverick's explanations, it has been suggested that, etymologically, his gobbledegook combined an Old French word for 'mouth' with 'gook', the latter reminiscent of 'goo', something sticky and murky. Gobbledegook therefore was something as unpleasant as muck coming out of the mouth of some people.

GO IN ONE EAR AND OUT OF THE OTHER

Nothing could express the ineffectiveness of a reprimand or admonition more clearly than the statement that its words 'go in one ear and out of the other'. But the choice of this metaphor has risky implications. Would it not suggest that whoever thus, contemptuously, pays no attention to whatever has been said, might do so because nothing—in the way of brains—separates his one ear from the other?

GOING FOR A SONG

Anything sold at a price far below its true value is described as 'going for a song'. The choice of words is based on an actual incident in the life of Edmund Spenser, who has been called the poet of poets of England.

Living during the reign of Elizabeth I, he dedicated his most famous work, *The Faerie Queene*, to her. He had composed it as an allegory in her praise. This so delighted the queen that she instructed her treasurer, William Cecil, the first Baron of Burleigh, to reward Spenser with a gift of £500. The baron, who was not kindly disposed towards Spenser, regarded the amount as exorbitant. It was much too large to be paid for just 'a song'. Accordingly, he reduced the suggested sum to £100.

His unilateral action, born out of spite, has been forgotten. However, 'going for a song', the phrase to which it gave birth, has survived his squalid deed.

Spenser died almost a pauper, having experienced much tragedy. But his place in the life of the nation and the world of literature was duly recognised. He was buried in Westminster Abbey, close to Chaucer, another of Britain's truly great figures of literature.

Going gaga

Those becoming mentally unbalanced are said to be 'going gaga'. The word 'gaga' itself has been explained as the result of a linguistic deterioration, though of which kind is not certain.

Some have traced it to *gâteau*, the French term for a senile person, no longer fully in control of body and mind. This distorted description may well have been the source of 'gaga'.

Rather unconvincing, though frequently repeated, is the claim that 'gaga' was first created in artistic circles by those who, unable to appreciate his new style, ridiculed Paul Gaugin, the (posthumously famous) painter. His was an unhappy life, particularly towards its end, and his demeanour then might have reflected the agony of his mind. Anything abnormal was said to be like Gaugin and his primitive, absurd and even 'barbaric' paintings. In its deplorable abuse, his name was eventually changed beyond recognition and, no longer identifiable with the man, became the present-day 'gaga'.

Perhaps none of these derivations is correct and 'gaga' neither (mis)represents a remarkable painter nor makes fun of the misery of geriatrics. An onomatopoeic word, it merely tries to imitate the sound of the idiotic laugh made by unfortunate people unkindly decried as imbeciles.

Gondola

The name gondola, as could be expected, is Venetian. A sixteenth-century dialect word, very appropriately, it is derived from an Italian root describing an early kind of rock and roll. It referred to the soothing motion experienced by travellers along the canals.

Puzzling is the fact that gondolas are painted black. Several reasons have been proffered. The original choice of the cheerless colour, one explanation has it, was far from dismal. It was pragmatic, selected by lovers who were very much concerned to keep their tryst in the dark! They seemed to be well camouflaged in a vessel so obscured.

Unfaithful husbands on their escapades during the night, it has been said, obviously wished to stay inconspicuous and incognito, lest their adultery be discovered and create a scandal. Therefore they had the gondolas in which they met their amour, literally, blacked out. It enabled them to float along unhurried, unharassed and—hopefully—undetected.

Far from happy, and even morbid, are other reasons given. They trace the black colour of the gondolas to the time when the plague reached Venice, and many of its citizens had fallen victim to the dreaded disease. The gondolas then served as much-needed hearses. In deference to the dead they carried and their mourners, they were painted black.

Still related to death is yet another claim. At the passing of a much beloved Doge, Venetians decided publicly to display their grief by painting all their boats black. And these have remained so ever since.

Whichever way, the puzzling black colour is a perpetual memorial, whether to loves long gone or lives lost.

GONE TO THE DOGS

Throughout history and all over the world, the dog has been man's constant companion. Loyal and brave, it has contributed to human welfare in the most varied ways—as a guard, a lifesaver, hunter and pet. Nevertheless and surprisingly, its influence on everyday phrases mainly reflects the seamy side of its life—and death.

In some countries and at various times dogs have been feared and shunned. And not without reason. Because dogs often carried rabies and tetanus, their bite could prove fatal. Starved, the poor creatures attacked the unwary. Reproducing fast, they were considered a nuisance, if not a threat. Chased away, they began to roam the outskirts of villages and settlements seeking food wherever they could find it, in dumps and among refuse. Not looked after like treasured pets, their life was a constant struggle.

In their desperate struggle to survive, they became bedraggled, diseased and ferocious. It was this existence of travail which—paradoxically—enriched the vocabulary in a number of metaphors. The depraved were called 'dirty dogs'. Those who had fallen on bad times were said to 'lead a dog's life' or, worse still, to have 'gone to the dogs'.

Reminiscent of the ultimate fate of such an abandoned canine, the most destitute and forgotten of persons was said to 'die like a dog'.

GOOD FOOTING

A pleasant relationship with other people, not least those in a superior position, is portrayed as being 'on a good footing' with them. It is a peculiar way of describing a close association. However, there seems to have been a good reason for doing so.

According to some, the phrase goes back to a practice of early apprenticeships. It was the custom on the first day at work for an apprentice to invite all their workmates for drinks. The new apprentice '*footed* the bill'. If proved a generous host, the apprentice made friends for keeps. The hospitality would never be forgotten. Recalling how much it had cost, it was said the novice gained 'a good footing'. Indeed, as it were, the apprentice had paid for entry into the craft. It gave them permission to put their *foot* into the workshop to learn the trade.

A second derivation links the phrase with an early and bizarre interpretation of human anatomy, the importance given to the length of one of man's digits! At one time, the dimension of the middle toes determined a person's 'standing' in the community. Thus, the measurement of their foot decided their status in the eyes of others. Those whom nature and genes had endowed with large feet were lucky to be 'on a good footing'. They were welcome and looked up to. How odd that people judged a person's rank by the size of their foot.

Grapevine

If a journalist receives information over the 'grapevine', on the 'bush telegraph' or (in recent jargon) by it having 'fallen off the back of a truck', it is mostly from sources he does not wish to disclose.

To begin with, however, hearing something on the grapevine meant for a rumour to travel at great speed—often from remote areas—as if along telegraph wires. It was in fact these very telegraph wires which, most likely, were responsible for the saying. In the early days, badly sagging, they reminded people of trailing grapevines.

The grapevine as a metaphor goes back to the American Civil War. It was then applied to unconfirmed news or mere rumours, exchanged between prisoners of war and their families or army groups. Frequently the information was of a secret nature. Therefore special efforts were made for it not to be discovered or intercepted. Illegal telegraph lines strung between the various points were accordingly camouflaged and, at times, made to look like vines. This, too, may account for the expression.

Green fingers and a green thumb

Those who have a knack for gardening and growing things are said to have green fingers or a green thumb. Their appraisal might quite easily be explained by natural causes, as the result of their preoccupation with verdure. Frequent handling of green plants has rubbed off the colour onto their hands, thus the description of having green fingers or a green thumb.

Even as a metaphor, it was well chosen and very much down to earth. Experienced gardeners when planting shoots press down the surrounding soil with their thumb or fingers, which helps young plants grow all the better.

A legend about an Italian monk reinforced what has become a figure of speech. Fra Antonio was admired by his brethren for the beauty of the garden he had planted. In spite of all possible efforts on their part, they could not equal it. Asking him for the secret, he was lost for an answer. Maybe, he humbly suggested, the reason was the special love he felt for the flowers.

Unconvinced, and without Antonio being aware of it, they watched him at work to discover that, indeed, he had a green thumb. Steeped in the supernatural, the monks firmly believed that his green thumb was a divine gift which mysteriously made Fra Antonio's plants and flowers thrive. Ever since, those like him, specially successful in making things grow and flourish, are thought to possess a God-given green thumb or green fingers.

GROOVY

Groovy is a word of modern coinage, meaning that something is 'with it', up-to-date and very exciting. It is the ultimate in enjoyment.

The word, though revived in the 1960s, goes back to the days of the early talking machine, the phonograph. This reproduced sound from a track indented into tin foil wrapped around a brass pipe, to be superseded by wax cylinders. Finally, these were replaced by grooved records. If the needle or stylus did not jump out of its track, it ran smoothly, literally it was 'in the groove'—groovy.

GUNG HO

Gung ho is pidgin English for 'to work together'. It is now used to express unbounded and, at times, excessive enthusiasm. The phrase is derived from the Mandarin Chinese *keng ho*, literally meaning 'more fiery'. That it was adopted into everyday language paradoxically was due both to religious leaders and a military commander.

Christian missionaries to China first chose the words (in the 1830s) as a most appropriate slogan for the industrial cooperatives they had established in the country. It seemed apt to inspire the people joining in the work to devote their efforts for the good of all, irrespective of their political views. *Gung ho*—'to work together'—was indeed the best assurance of success.

Whilst being assigned as an observer to the Chinese army, Lieutenant Colonel (later General) Evans F. Carlson picked up the slogan. He immediately was impressed by it, so much so that when he was appointed head of the American Marines, he made it their motto. Most likely, it contributed to the successful outcome of a significant mission he led during the Second World War. The division had been given orders to destroy the radio station on the then Japanese-occupied Makin, an atoll situated at the northern end of Gilbert Island in the west of the Pacific Ocean. Carlson completed his mission within 48 hours (on 18–19 August 1942), rendering the island militarily useless for the rest of the war.

No doubt Carlson had inspired his marines by the slogan he had made their own. Gung ho soon became known far beyond the war zone. Popularised in the following year by a film called after it, gung ho found its lasting place in the English language meaning fiery enthusiasm.

Halcyon Days

Halcyon days are happy, calm, and peaceful days. Originally, they referred specifically to the seven days that preceded and followed the shortest day of the year. According to ancient fable, during that period the seas are calm and safest for navigation. Even the birds knew this, especially the kingfisher, known in Greek as *halcyon*. Wisely taking advantage of the tranquil sea and its unruffled waters, it built a floating nest on the swells in which it could safely lay and hatch its eggs.

In fact, the bird's very name recalls the legend, though in an abbreviated form. It combines the Greek *hals*, for 'the sea', with *kuon*, to 'brood on' or to 'conceive'.

Happy as Larry

Obviously, to be as 'happy as Larry' referred to some popular figure, renowned for his blissful cheerfulness.

'Larry' (Laurence) Foley (1849–1917), an Australian champion boxer, is thought to have been this very person. One of the best-known sportsmen in the country in the 1870s, he also ran a Sydney hotel and a boxing school. His exhibitions and prize fights attracted vast crowds.

On a visit to Sydney, a famous English pugilist, after a memorable encounter with Larry, proclaimed him publicly as the best man in the world for his weight (185 kilograms (410 pounds) at the time). Everyone knew and admired Larry, not least his zest for life and his pleasant disposition.

During his time, he followed (and attempted) many other pursuits. Early on, in fact, he had been the leader of a notorious gang in the Sydney slums.

He had worked as a builder's labourer and been appointed the official demolition contractor of New South Wales. At one time he even considered standing for parliament. No wonder that to be 'as happy as Larry' became a phrase that outlived the boxer.

It is only proper to add that sceptics have doubted the identification. They say that, though Larry Foley seemed so ideal to fill the bill, most likely the 'happy Larry' had never been a real person, but was merely a figment of imagination.

'HAPPY BIRTHDAY TO YOU'

'Happy Birthday to You' is one of the most frequently sung songs of all time, and has become part of almost every birthday celebration—once even in space!

The story of its creation is linked with the advanced teaching methods of a young American pioneer of modern pedagogics. Patty Hill was twenty-one years old when, in 1889, she graduated from the Kindergarten Teachers Training College in Louisville, Kentucky. Her great abilities and progressive views on education had not gone unnoticed by the principal. He felt that it would be of great advantage to the College to retain her services. Patty gladly accepted his offer to become head of the College infants school, knowing that she would be given every support in implementing some of her novel ideas. On her appointment, she was joined at the school by her sister Mildred, a music teacher.

Patty was convinced that for a school to be truly successful, it had to be a cheerful place. Only a joyful and relaxed atmosphere could bring out the best from teachers and pupils. Most of all, Patty believed in teaching by song.

To put her idea into practice, she published, jointly with her sister, *Song Stories for the Kindergarten and Primary Schools*. Patty wrote the words and Mildred set them to music. Of all the songs in the collection, their favourite was 'Good Morning to All'. It was intended to be sung at the beginning of every school day:

Good morning to you
Good morning to you,
Good morning, dear children
Good morning to all.

While retaining the melody, Patty one day changed the lyrics! She replaced them with the now well-known words of 'Happy Birthday to You'! They were to be sung on the birthday of every pupil.

An instant success, the song soon spread beyond the confines of the school. Its very simplicity and directness appealed to people of all ages. The song became the property of the world. In fact, it was only in 1934 that a publisher persuaded the sisters to copyright it.

'Happy Birthday to You' has yet another distinction. It became the first song to be sung in space. On 8 March 1969, the astronauts on Apollo IX sang it to celebrate the birthday of Christopher Kraft, at that time director of NASA space operations.

HARPING

To dwell on a topic unendingly or to refer to it so often that to listen to it becomes tedious is described as 'harping'.

It seems an unkind use of the instrument that from very early days has added so much beauty to the world of music and whose play, as the Bible tells, soothed King Saul during his bouts of melancholy.

The derogatory idiom recalls a practice of Victorian times. To entertain guests, the daughter of the house was called upon to display her (at times very mediocre) musical talents in giving a recital on the harp. Her very limited repertoire was confined to well-known tunes. It often became an ordeal for the captive audience who had politely to endure her 'harping'.

It has also been said that the phrase was prompted by thinking of someone harping the same string 'again and again'.

HAVE A LOT OF GALL

An early medical misdiagnosis might well be responsible for speaking of people who are of a pushy, arrogant and outright insolent nature as having 'a lot of gall'.

Gall, an alternate name for bile, originally described its yellow colour. Medieval anatomists wrongly assumed that if produced in too great a quantity by the liver, it would affect a person's entire character. Those suffering from such excess of bile, by absorbing it into their body, would acquire an equally sour temperament. Through no fault of their own, therefore, for mere physical reasons, they became cantankerous, ill-humoured and aggressive. It was all the result of their overactive liver.

HAVE SOMETHING UP ONE'S SLEEVE

Those who have a surprise in store are said to 'have something up their sleeve'. The figure of speech may recall the popular conjurers' trick to produce 'out of the air' a rabbit and all kinds of objects. Obviously, they had them hidden up their sleeve.

More likely and making even better sense, the phrase might go back to the early days of men's fashion, when the sleeves of their coats were wide and long, as they still are on an academic gown. When so desired or needed, for instance in windy and rainy weather, the sleeves could be fastened around the wrist by means of buttons specially provided for the purpose. Though still retained on men's jackets these buttons are useless now. With pockets rare or non-existent at the time, it was so easy to have something hidden up one's sleeve.

HAWKER

The hawker's name describes a feature of the early way of trade. Going from place to place, they often carried wares on their backs, which would become bent by the load. Or the trader might squat down to sell his goods.

Derived from the German *hocken*, the hawker portrays either practice. In German the word was used both for 'bending down' (*niederhocken*) and the description of old people who walked with a stoop.

There is no truth in the suggestion also made that, originally, a *hawk*er was an itinerant dealer in foreign hawks, making their way from castle to castle.

HIGH HEELS

Strangely, high heels in Europe became the fashion not through a woman but a man. And, as so often in the world of fashion, France set the trend.

With all his grandeur, Louis XIV, the sun king, had been bereft by nature of physical stature, being merely 1.57 metres (5.2 feet) tall. A vain man, he was very conscious of his lack of height. He became specially aware of it on state occasions, when mingling with his subjects and dignatories. They were able to look down on him, something which he felt was not only most inappropriate, but humiliating. For this reason he had high heels made for his shoes, which he wore at all such functions.

Royalty has always set the fashion, and once women learned of the king's elevation (of his shoes), they lost no time in having high heels made for themselves, which even the men adopted, at least for some time. They abandoned them when, no longer riding on horseback, they were too uncomfortable to walk in. Women, however, retained them. In their pursuit to be deemed fashionable, they were prepared to suffer or even to do harm to their feet and back.

HIS NAME IS MUD

Unfortunate circumstances linked with a tragedy in American history gave rise to the defamatory expression that 'his name is mud'. The mud spoken of, however, is not ordinary dirt but a man's name.

On the night of President Lincoln's assassination, a peace-loving country doctor in southern Maryland, Dr Samuel A. Mudd, treated an injured traveller. He was completely unaware of the man's identity and that, in fact, he was the assassin John Wilkes Booth who, only a few hours previously, had killed the president. While making his escape from the scene of the murder, Ford's Theater, Washington, DC, a spur on his boot had been caught in one of the flags decorating the presidential box, causing a fracture of one of his legs.

Dr Mudd, after setting and bandaging Booth's injured limb, let him and the friend accompanying him stay in his home overnight. It was only on the following morning that Dr Mudd heard of the assassination and, his suspicions aroused, immediately informed the authorities of what had occurred.

Nonetheless, he was arrested, subsequently to be tried by a military court. All Mudd had done was an innocent act of mercy and his duty as a doctor. But in the eyes of a vengeful prosecution and of a grieving nation, embittered to the point of hysteria, he was an accomplice in the conspiracy. In their minds, he had committed treason. He was sentenced to a life of hard labour and, in chains, taken to Fort Jefferson, the country's most notorious prison. Overnight 'his name is Mudd' became a contemptuous charge.

There is no doubt that this tragic incident made the phrase known worldwide. However, with the passing of years, its origin was forgotten and Mudd's name changed into mere 'mud'.

Some authorities feel that, although Dr Mudd's sad fate popularised the phrase, it had existed for many centuries. Mud, being dirty, obviously soiled people. It could do so both by splattering them in the street or, figuratively speaking, by besmirching their character by scandalous accusations. Long before the American Civil War, newspapers which made it their business to slander men's names were referred to as the 'mud press'.

HOBNOB

Hobnobbing, today solely used to describe persons 'rubbing shoulders' with people of superior standing, has a much more egalitarian background.

The phrase to 'hobnob' can be traced to English inns and public houses of the 1700s. Anyone invited to hobnob was asked to join in having a glass of beer. This could be obtained either warm or cold. In winter the beer was warmed up by letting it stand on a sort of grate inside a fireplace, which was known as the 'hob'. With refrigeration still unknown cold beer was served at room temperature. The filled mugs were kept standing on a table which was referred to as a 'nob'. When offering a beer to his guest, the host inquired which of the two was preferred, 'hob or nob'.

Drinking together created good fellowship. This ultimately developed close relationships and familiarity. Using a contracted version of the hob and the nob, those concerned were soon said to 'hobnob'. The term eventually was no longer confined to ale houses or drinking, but generally indicated socialising, being on intimate terms.

An alternate derivation, going back to Shakespearean times, claims that the term is a corruption of the Anglo-Saxon 'hab nab'—'to have' and 'not to have' something. Soon this took on the meaning of 'give and take'. It pointed to an easy-going friendship of those hobnobbing. Treating each other with a drink in turn, in the very sense of the Australian 'shout', they became true mates.

HOCK

Though nowadays an entire group of German white wines (initially known as 'Rhenish') is referred to as 'hock', originally this was one specific brand.

The name is derived from that of Hochheim, a German city on the Main. Situated near the river's confluence with the Rhine, it is the centre of an entire region noted for the growing and producing of some of the best white wines. Not surprisingly therefore, people called them after the town, the 'Hochheimers'. A long name, they soon cut it short. Merely retaining its first syllable, they changed the Hochheimer into the 'Hoch'.

The English took a liking to the wine, not least so Queen Victoria. No doubt it was a taste she had acquired through Prince Albert, her German-born husband. To voice the guttural 'ch' of Hoch (very much like the 'ch' of the Scottish 'loch') was beyond the English tongues. They thus smoothed the hard sound to that of a 'k' and thereby changed the *hoch* into *hock*, by which name the drink has been known ever since.

As if to confuse the issue, another claim has been made. It denies any connection of the name with that of the city and asserts its independent existence from the very beginning.

Hoch is the German for 'high' and the German toast, equivalent to the English 'he is a jolly good fellow', chanted that 'high (hoch) shall he live, three times high' (Hoch soll er leben, dreimal hoch). The 'high' in this context was equivalent to 'long' and 'noble'. As, traditionally, a toast is made with a glass of white wine, the drink was soon identified with the first word of the felicitation and thus became the 'hoch'.

HOLY SMOKE

'Holy smoke', now a mild swear word, used harmlessly as an expression of intense amazement, originally had sacred associations. In the early days to refer to it lightly and in a mundane situation was regarded as totally out of place and highly offensive, quite literally profane.

Smoke—as from a furnace—ascended from Mount Sinai, when God revealed the Ten Commandments (Ex. 19:18). A pillar of cloud looking like smoke preceded the Israelites on their wanderings through the wilderness as a guide and a guardian (Ex. 13:21).

Smoke, like a prayer, rose heavenwards from the altars of the sanctuary on which the priests burnt the offerings of the people and the incense. In each case it was 'holy smoke' which, to make use of in everyday conversation, was regarded as blasphemous.

HONEYMOON DESTINATION— WHY IT IS KEPT SECRET

Many a newly wed couple do not like to reveal, even to their closest friends, the place where they are going to spend their honeymoon. They really do not know why they keep it a secret and mostly, superstitiously, believe it to be for good luck. The practice has also been rationalised by the explanation that they want to be left alone and, by the added air of secrecy, make the occasion all the more romantic.

Actually, the custom originated in the days when the man used to capture his bride-to-be. There was every reason, therefore, for the couple not to make known their whereabouts, lest the woman's family catch up with them and create unpleasantness or, at the very worst, take the woman back. Once the honeymoon was over, the young couple hoped, tempers would have cooled and the new situation would be accepted.

HOODLUM

The hoodlum is a social phenomenon found in many countries, and it is no wonder therefore that the origin of this name has had a variety of explanations.

It is perhaps the result of a printer's error in a San Francisco paper in the early 1870s. At the time, a gang of thugs made life in that city very unpleasant. In search of an apt description, a reporter made use of their leader's name, which was Muldoon.

To make his coinage more memorable, he reversed the name and referred to the hooligans as 'noodlums'. When printing the report, the typesetter mistook the initial 'n' for an 'h' and thus, by mere error, introduced the 'hoodlum', a word and designation which has never been corrected. From the San Francisco region it spread to all English-speaking people.

Another version gives the account a slightly different slant, and is more plausible. There was no mistake on the part of the typesetter and the reporter had in fact called the gang by its leader's name, without changing it in any way. However, his editor, afraid of retaliatory action from the gang, though using their leader's name, cleverly changed it—he hoped beyond recognition. For this reason, he spelled Muldoon's name back to front and, further to camouflage it, replaced the 'n' with an 'h'—with the resultant hoodlum.

Other derivations cite (South) German and Swiss roots, particularly a Bavarian slang word for ruffians.

It has also been said that the hoodlum embodies the gangsters' cry when attacking their victims, 'huddle 'em!'

Hoo-ha

Hoo-ha, as a slang word for a rowdy, noisy argument or lots of fuss and bother, may well be an imitation of the raucous noise it creates. As philologists would say, this is an onomatopoeic term.

Yet it has also been suggested to come from the Yiddish language to be popularised by comedians both on radio and television, particularly in the United States. In its Yiddish connotation, it is a multipurpose exclamation which can indicate a whole spectrum of human sentiments and attitudes. Hoo-ha can express excitement, admiration, jealousy and surprise. Which of these it is depends on one's tone of voice and facial expression.

Horned helmets

A distinguishing feature of early armour was the horned helmet, best known through the portrayal of Viking warriors. It is often incorrectly assumed they were worn to frighten the enemy by simulating a charging bull or deer. They developed from an earlier custom, steeped in occult tradition. Fighters used to don the skin of an animal, with the horns still attached to it. The animal's power and aggressiveness, they believed, would be magically transferred to them.

HULLABALOO

'Hullabaloo' is a tumultuous noise, with a variety of assumed origins and alternative renderings.

Some recognise in the word the imitation of the sound of howling wind or of a roaring crowd. In other versions it appeared as hurley-bolloo and, immortalised by Shakespeare's witches in Macbeth, as hurly-burly.

An Irish ancestry has been suggested too. Hullabaloo copied the sound of wailing that accompanied Irish burials and was part of their wakes.

The English linked it with death of a different kind. They traced hullabaloo to an imitation of 'halloo', the hunters' cry with which they urged on their hounds to chase the quarry. This 'halloo', most likely, had developed out of an earlier shout of 'hare' or 'haro', as it was specifying the animal.

The hullabaloo has also been cited as a typical example of rhyming reduplication, the echoing of the uproar made by people—their halloo...

Another meaning serves to confuse rather than clarify. The confusion comes from an interpretation which expresses a real contradiction of terms. Hullabaloo, it said, was a combination of 'hello' called out to get attention and (the Scottish) *baloo* for a 'lullaby'. If true, it would present the oddest of mixtures.

HUNKY-DORY (HONKY-DORY)

The pleasing affirmation that everything is 'hunky-dory' has been traced to different parts of the world.

No matter how far people travel and how much they enjoy their trip, they are always happy when safely returning 'home', known in Dutch as *honk*. Honky reflected their joyful contentment. Extended to 'honky-dory', it became even more expressive of their feeling that everything (now) was fine.

'Honk' is also the name of the goal in the game of tag. The first to reach it was 'home' and had every reason to be happy. They had won the game.

Hunky-dory is a peculiar phrase and might very likely be the result of corrupted speech. This would tally with an explanation linking the words with American sailors. They are said to have picked the phrase up as an odd kind of memento when their ship called in at Yokohama, Japan. After spending so much time at sea, sailors are always happy to make port and to seek 'relaxation and recreation'. This they often do in the red-light district of the city. Thus when an American naval unit docked at Yokohama, the men made their way straight to the area where the 'ladies of the night' were waiting, in and around a street named Huncho-dori. Strategically positioned, it was not far from the ship and the sailors had no difficulty in finding their way back.

Recalling the location later and the good time they had enjoyed there, they spoke of how everything had been 'hunky-dory', slightly changing the name of the Japanese city street of pleasant memories.

Honky-dory has also been understood to be indigenously American. It has been linked with the Civil War and a song popular at the time, 'Josephus Orange Blossom'. One of its catchy lines spoke of the red-hot honky-dory contraband. No one before had ever heard anything like this. It helped people remember the words all the more and use them on every possible occasion. Once hostilities had ceased and when the song was forgotten, 'honky-dory' remained ingrained in popular speech. It denoted the delight that things were going really well, just as it had once expressed people's satisfaction on the arrival of contraband goods.

HYPOCHONDRIAC

An apocryphal story tells of a headstone which, at the specific wish of the woman whose grave it marked, carried the inscription, 'I told you I was sick.' From beyond the grave, the deceased reprimanded people for having disbelieved her genuine complaints of ill-health.

To be called a hypochondriac nowadays suggests someone's abnormal anxieties about their health, imagining that they suffer from a disease which has no organic basis. It is all in the mind, it is said.

The very name of hypochondria shows that early doctors saw in the patient's condition an actual physical malfunction. The hypochondriac thus is the victim of both imagined bad health and its misdiagnosis. The description—from the Greek—locates the cause of the affliction 'under the ribs' (combining the Greek *hypo* for 'under' with *khondros*, for 'cartilage'). It was (wrongly) assumed that vapours from that part of the body caused the patient's illusion.

ICED TEA
IMBECILE
INFANT
INGRAINED
IN-LAWS
IRISH COFFEE

ICED TEA

It so happened that both iced tea and tea bags were introduced to the world by the United States in 1904.

An English exhibitor at the World Fair then held at St Louis, Missouri, sold tea he had imported from the Far East. To promote the product, he cleverly offered free cups of hot tea. However, his well-laid plans went awry. In the heat of summer, no visitor to the Fair fancied his samples.

An enterprising merchant, the Englishman did not give up easily. Observant as well, he soon noticed how people enjoyed the iced refreshments served at neighbouring stalls. This gave him the idea to cool down his hot tea with ice cubes and offer it as a novel refreshing drink.

No sooner thought than done. The experiment paid off and his iced tea caught on. In fact, a weight-conscious clientele welcomed a beverage which was not only low in temperature and in price, but also in calories.

IMBECILE

Today an imbecile is an intellectually handicapped person. This has not always been the case. The word comes from a combination of the Latin *in* used in the sense of 'on', and *baculum* for a 'rod' or a 'stick', therefore literally meaning 'on a stick'. A physically handicapped person, when moving about, needed the aid of a crutch. Around the seventeenth century the term was transferred from the physically impeded to the feeble in mind.

Oddly, imbecile thus carries the same root as the bacillus, so called because some bacteria, when seen under the microscope, are rod-shaped.

INFANT

An infant is so called because a young child does not speak. Infant joins the Latin negative *in* with *fari*, the Latin for 'speak'. Literally therefore, an infant is 'speechless'. Hence, if taken seriously, no child should be called an infant from the moment it starts to speak.

INGRAINED

Something which completely and irremovably belongs to an object or a character is called 'ingrained'. This figure of speech in a single word does not, as might be imagined, relate to the grain in wood which penetrates it throughout. It is derived from *granum*, the Latin for both a grain of wheat, a seed, and the name of an insect from whose dried body the Romans produced a fast red dye. This was also known as cochineal from the Greek *kokkos*, for a 'berry', for which the insect was first mistaken.

'Ingrained' therefore once referred to something so thoroughly dyed that nothing could ever change its colour or cause it to fade. Shakespeare used the metaphor in *Twelfth Night* when Olivia says, "Tis in graine, Sir; 'twill endure wind and weather.'

IN-LAWS

When getting married, one acquires not only a mother and father-in-law, but many other in-laws as well.

It is generally assumed that although not blood-related, the spouse's mother and father have become parents 'in law', meaning according to the common law of the country. This is incorrect, and the term is misleading and needs qualification. The lawful part within the relationship does not bestow any legal standing.

The law referred to is the canon law of the Church of England, the ecclesiastical rules and regulations concerning 'Kindred and Affinity', as tabulated at the end of the *Book of Common Prayer*.

IRISH COFFEE

Surprisingly, Irish coffee is not only a gift of the Emerald Isle to the world, to add to its enjoyment in food and drink, but part of the history of aviation. It was created in the 1950s, at Shannon airport on the west coast of Ireland, and was the result of early trans-Atlantic flights.

At the time, the quantity of fuel aircraft could carry was just sufficient for the long stretch between the United States and the Irish coast. This made it necessary for all planes to stop over at Shannon to refuel. Tired and exhausted from the then still long and wearisome flight, both crew and passengers could well do with a 'pick-up'. Joe Sheridan, the airport's barman, was quick to come to the rescue. He served the arrivals a strong cup of coffee. To fortify it, he added a dash of whiskey, topping his novel concoction with whipped cream. It was the birth of Irish coffee and immediately caught on.

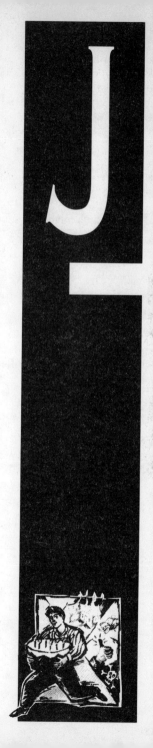

JACKKNIFE

It would be easy to imagine that a jackknife is so called because it is such a handy tool for anyone—any Jack. People can carry it safely in their pockets wherever they go as its sharp edge is sheathed when not in use. However, it has been claimed (in 1776) that its description was chosen in honour of its inventor, allegedly Jacques de Liège, a cutler.

The Scots corrupted his name (and the knife) into *jockteleg*, which gave the English the now obsolete *jackleg*.

JACUZZI

Several factors combined in the invention of the jacuzzi, a whirlpool bath. It is named after Candido Jacuzzi, an Italian immigrant to the United States.

Born in the village of Casarsa del Friuli, in a poor farming region of northeast Italy, Candido was the youngest of seven brothers who, with six sisters, came to America in 1905. Settling in Berkeley, they purchased a small machine shop, establishing a family firm, known as Jacuzzi Brothers. To start with, they manufactured agricultural machinery and—taking advantage of the emerging aero-industry—aircraft. The Jacuzzi propeller, nicknamed the Jacuzzi 'toothpick', was used by the United States and allied forces during the First World War. However, the death of one of the brothers (in 1921) due to a crash in one of their planes, on their mother's suggestion, made them switch to another, much less perilous, industrial venture—the manufacture of hydraulic pumps.

Candido's son was afflicted with rheumatoid arthritis, just when doctors had realised the great value of hydrotherapy. This made Candido feel that hydro-massage might be of benefit in the treatment of his son. But, at the time, only large communal tubs in hospitals and spas could provide it.

He felt that this could be done at home as well, and thus he installed a jet pump into their bath. The invention became known as the jacuzzi.

When further developed and improved, the 'hot tub' as 'jacuzzi' became a craze in the 1950s, making its production a multi-million-dollar enterprise. What had been a personal misfortune created a veritable fortune for the family firm.

Candido died at the ripe old age of 83 in 1986. Though paralysed then, he could look back on a phenomenal career, and how an Italian country boy's name had become a household word.

JEEP

It is an unfortunate paradox that the exigencies of war have always spurred the inventive genius of people. War provided the incentive (and governments the funds) for numerous innovations, discoveries and improvements which, subsequently, in peacetime, enriched life. The jeep is such a child of war.

A powerful, versatile four-wheel-drive vehicle, it was first constructed for the American forces in the Second World War. As it was to serve as a general purpose vehicle, the military authorities referred to it as such. However, for the sake of brevity, they substituted for the ponderous designation two letters, GP, its initials. Some of the early models are said to have had them already painted on their bodies.

Nevertheless, to begin with, the soldiers were not sure what to call it. This made them dub the car with a colourful variety of names. They called it the 'blitz buggy', the 'command-reconnaissance car' and, as it could carry four men, the 'quad car'. However, none of the names really fitted or caught on.

Imaginatively, the men then combined the letters GP. Making out of them a new word, they coined the 'jeep'. Not being linguists, they were not bound by laws of language or spelling. Their transformation of the 'g' into a 'j' was not due to slovenly speech or faulty spelling. It was the result of the men's love of 'Popeye the Sailor', then one of the most popular comic strips. One of its figures, it is assumed, actually influenced them in their choice of name.

Elzie Crisler Segar, who had first created the comic strip in 1930, on 16 March 1936 added to it yet another character. It was a small mystical animal, endowed with supernatural power. In the cartoon it was delivered to Popeye in a box. Segar called it 'Eugene the Jeep'. The odd creature could do almost anything and made the chirping sound of 'jeep', no doubt responsible for its description.

The widely-syndicated cartoon was well-known to the soldiers, and so was the 'jeep'. It did not take them long to bestow its name on the powerful car which, like the creature, was most versatile.

JINX

People who have a run of bad luck might say that there must be a jinx on them. In so doing, they perpetuate the ancient occult belief in the malevolent power of the wryneck. The bird, related to the woodpecker, was known in Greek as *yinx*.

The bird possibly asked for its evil reputation by a peculiar habit. When disturbed, it twists its neck in the strangest way. Another of its features which might well have further contributed to the bird's imagined supernatural connection was its plumage. Of mottled grey and brown, it serves as a perfect camouflage. As a result, it frequently happened that though being heard, it could not be seen. No wonder then that the wryneck became part of witchcraft and was used for charms, spells and aphrodisiac potions.

Luckily for the creature, its association with the netherworld has been forgotten. With its Greek name being misspelled beyond recognition, it is well concealed. No one would recognise its presence in a jinx.

JOYSTICK

'Joystick' is an intriguing term pilots once colloquially used for the stick with which they controlled the aircraft.

Though at times interpreted in an obscene sense, the origin of its description might be quite innocuous. Some say it reflects the joy it gave to the pilots by enabling them by slightly moving the stick to change the course of the flight, its altitude and direction. Others believed that the name was suggested by the vibrations of the stick. Recalling human body language, the pilot compared it to someone so exhilarated that they were shaking with joy.

JUGGERNAUT

Metaphorically, a juggernaut is a tremendous force, irresistibly moving on and crushing everything in its way.

Now a figure of speech, it perpetuates a ritual once part of Hindu worship of the god Vishnu. In one of his manifold manifestations he was known as Jagannatha, the Sanskrit for 'the lord of the universe', the English juggernaut.

An annual festival in his honour was celebrated at the famous shrine of Puri in Orissa, India. On the occasion, his image, of gigantic size (13.5 metres (45 feet) in height and 2.1 metres (7 feet) across), was placed on a vehicle equally enormous in dimension and rebuilt every year. Each of its 16 large wheels, made of solid wood, measured almost 2.1 metres in diameter. In a procession the wagon was dragged along by means of ropes, with pilgrims vying with each other to undertake this most onerous task. Many of the volunteers collapsed from exhaustion, some of them fatally.

Countless devout Hindu believers crowded around the cart and accompanied it on its way. Some of them, so tradition tells, overcome by religious frenzy, threw themselves under the moving vehicle to be crushed by its heavy wheels. They are said to have done so happily, in the belief that their sacrificial death would bring to an end their ceaseless cycle of birth and death, attaining for them instant and eternal bliss.

Though, during their rule of India, the British stopped the practice, the memory of the juggernaut did not die. It became a picture of a force, ruthless and relentless in its progress, and as such joined the vocabulary.

Far removed from the religious association, in England a juggernaut also describes a large transport vehicle, used to carry heavy loads over vast distances.

KAMIKAZE ATTACKS
KEEP AN EAR TO THE GROUND
KEEP AT BAY
KEEP YOUR SHIRT ON
KICKBACKS
KILL TIME
KINK IN THE SIAMESE CAT'S TAIL
KISS BETTER
KIT AND CABOODLE
KNOCK ONE UP
KNOCK THE SPOTS OFF
KNUCKLE UNDER

Kamikaze attacks

Suicidal missions undertaken by Japanese pilots during the Second World War became known as kamikaze attacks. The Japanese word literally means 'divine wind'. The description can be traced to the end of the thirteenth century when in 1281 the Mongols, then at the very height of their power, tried to invade Japan.

Twice their attempts failed. On each occasion, the Mongolian fleet which had embarked on the mission was stopped, finally to be wiped out by devastating typhoons. Japanese people at the time were convinced that it was the result of divine intervention. Thus they called the typhoon a 'divine wind', *kami kaze* in their tongue. (It is interesting to note that, in modern terminology, a disastrous cyclone is still referred to as 'an act of God'.)

In the Second World War the Japanese military power formed the famous suicide squads in which pilots had to crash their planes, loaded with explosives, on selected targets. To enthuse the men chosen for the mission and make them feel that their tragic task was a godly deed, the authorities called it by the ancient name—*kamikaze*.

Keep an ear to the ground

A well-informed and alert person, always watching out for any sudden changes, developments or surprises, is said to keep an ear to the ground. The phrase is derived from a practice attributed to American Indians. Endowed with an acute sense of hearing, they would put their ear to the ground, enabling them to hear the approach of an enemy still outside their range of vision. By the vibrations of the ground, they could also tell the number of horses and their distance.

KEEP AT BAY

People had observed that bay trees never seemed to be struck by lightning. This could not be accidental, they reasoned, but—believing in the occult—must be the result of some supernatural power the tree possessed. This gave it not only immunity to thunderbolts, but endowed its foliage, berries and roots with the gift to act as a potent antidote against a multitude of dangers.

For their own protection, people thus planted bay trees near their homes. During thunderstorms, they put some of the leaves on their head and used the foliage as a repellent against poisonous snakes, witches, demons and other nefarious forces. Convinced of its curative properties, they used parts of the plant to heal consumption, liver complaints and even ease the effects of the plague. Most possibly, it was out of a combination of these superstitions and practices that the phrase to 'keep at bay' evolved. After all, as Einstein once remarked, 'imagination is more important than knowledge'.

Belief in the tree's potency is rooted in ancient myth. Greek legend tells how, to rescue his daughter Daphne from Apollo's pursuit, the river god Peneus had changed her into a bay tree. Romans believed a withering bay tree was an omen of death.

There is also the view that the phrase may embody the remnant of *abayer*, an Old French word. This spoke of the 'barking' or 'growling' of a dog which, most certainly, would keep an attacker at a safe distance—at bay.

KEEP YOUR SHIRT ON

Fashion has not only determined our dress, but it has also left an imprint on our way of speaking. During the last century, men's shirts had stiffly starched fronts. Though looking elegant, they constricted the wearer's movements. So attired, it would be very difficult for him and disadvantageous to engage in fisticuffs, not uncommon at the time. To do so successfully, he had to remove his shirt first.

When a heated argument threatened to get out of hand and develop into a physical fight, an opponent anxious to avoid it called on his adversary to keep his shirt on.

A very practical advice, it has now entered the realm of metaphors. It is used when trying to pacify and calm down someone highly agitated or in a belligerent mood.

KICKBACKS

Kickbacks, symptomatic of a corrupt society, have almost become an accepted practice in many walks of life.

Originally an American term, it goes back to the days of sailing vessels, when their captains were grossly underpaid and therefore forced somehow to supplement their meagre earnings. All at sea as it were, to make some extra money, they came to a private agreement with the provider of the goods their ships carried. Working hand in glove with them, they 'kicked back' into the stores of these merchants cargo destined to go on board. Literally, they 're-stored' the goods and, in reward, split their value with the double-dealing 'suppliers'.

KILL TIME

People speak of 'killing time' when forced to idle away precious hours, waiting for something or somebody.

The origin of the phrase is obscure. It was thieves' jargon, it has been suggested. They applied it—much less deadly—to wasting time.

According to others, at first there was nothing homicidal in the expression, not even figuratively. Its present-day murderous part is based on a mistake, a mix-up of words. The original saying did not refer to killing at all, but to early potters' kilns. Restricted in size, these could only process a limited number of items at a time. Thus potters were forced to interrupt their work frequently, waiting for the wares in their kiln to be ready, then to be replaced by the next batch to be fired.

They referred to this enforced interim as the 'kiln time'. Not to sit around doing nothing, the potters occupied themselves with odd jobs, of not much consequence. It did not take long for the 'kiln time' to be corrupted into 'killing time', a phrase that has been kept alive ever since.

KINK IN THE SIAMESE CAT'S TAIL

A Siamese cat with its outstanding features—the raucous voice, blue and sometimes crossed eyes—is most distinctive and different.

Folklore explains the conspicuous kink in its tail. It tells of a Thai princess and her pet Siamese cat which was her constant companion. One day, when about to take a bath in the river, the princess was concerned about the many precious rings on her hands, afraid that she might lose them in the water. To prevent this from happening, she removed the rings from her fingers and slipped them on to the tail of her faithful cat, and to secure them, she tied a knot. Ever since, the legend claims, Siamese felines have kept the kink in their tails.

KISS BETTER

Frequently, when a child has hurt itself and starts crying, its mother will try to soothe it by saying, 'I'll kiss it better.' Several reasons may have prompted the practice.

No doubt the display of love, concern and tenderness shown by the parent in itself will lessen the pain.

The kissing of the wound also recalls an early and effective method in the treatment of injuries. It is responsible for the well-known saying which speaks of someone lying low and licking their wounds. Animals instinctively do so. Apart from cleaning the sore, saliva has healing properties.

Those bitten by a venomous snake have learnt the benefit of sucking out the poison from the wound. Inevitably, the action became associated with kissing something better.

A religious tradition reinforced the belief. It tells how on a visit to Paris, fourteenth-century St Martin, Bishop of Tours, took pity on a leper he found sitting at the city gates. In deep compassion, he went up to him and kissed his sores. Instantly and miraculously, the man was cured.

KIT AND CABOODLE

Although to speak of the whole 'caboodle' refers already to the entire lot, to enlarge the phrase to 'kit and caboodle', if possible makes it even more embracing.

Kit is a shortened form of the kitbag, a knapsack in which soldiers packed and carried their eating utensils and other essentials. It is said to have evolved from the Dutch *kitte*, a box made of wooden staves in which workmen kept their tools. On the other hand, people have been suggested as its source—one's kith. After all, one's kith (and kin) are all the family and friends.

Caboodle, too, might be a combination of the kit with boodle, slightly disfigured in the fusion. Boodle has been derived as well from the Dutch *bodel*, used for 'property' and 'moveable goods'. Others traced it to an Old English word, designating a 'bundle' or a 'bunch'.

Kit and caboodle thus expressed an all-comprehensive collection, everything and everyone, linguistically still more closely drawn together by its alliteration.

KNOCK ONE UP

Bernard Shaw's observation that the only thing that divides the British from the Americans is their language is well known. Their different interpretation of a phrase or expression may become a source of embarrassment. A striking illustration is to 'knock one up'.

The American connotation of the idiom is to make a woman pregnant. Oddly, this retains the early English meaning of the words. In Shakespearean times 'knock' described the penis. In modern English, as spoken by the British, however, to 'knock one up' merely suggests waking up a person by knocking on the door.

The expression itself is part of English social history. In the early days of the Lancashire textile industry, those employed at the mills had to work from early morning till late at night, returning home totally exhausted. They could easily oversleep next morning. To make sure that they turned up at the factory on time, led to the introduction of a simple practice. Before sunrise, men walked through the streets of the city, equipped with a long stave. This they banged against the workers' bedroom windows, mostly situated on the upper floor. 'Knocking them up', they made certain that they were not late for work.

Working hours are now regulated by law. But, as a memento of the sweat labour, to 'knock up' has become an integral part of the English vocabulary, though now used merely metaphorically in an innocuous and harmless sense of being awakened.

KNOCK THE SPOTS OFF

If you 'knock the spots off' an opponent, in either a contest or a fight, you defeat them soundly.

The phrase might be connected with early shooting contests, in which playing cards were used as the target. Whoever was able to hit or 'knock off' its pips—the 'spots'—proved the best shot.

Another explanation relates the expression to boxing. Anyone knocked about was hit hard. Some unfortunates suffered brain injuries. Others, more lucky, merely saw spots in front of their eyes. As a figure of speech, it indicated that their opponent had taken the 'stuffing' out of them.

Initially, the saying might have been used much more literally. It could have suggested that the winner had thrashed his sparring partner so thoroughly that he knocked even the freckles—the spots—off his face.

Knuckle under

Those who yield to superior power are said to 'knuckle under'. The phrase recalls a former gesture of submission. The knuckle described not only the finger joints, but also those of the knees. Hence, to 'knuckle under' referred to people who went down on their knees, assuming an inferior position not only physically, but expressed in body language. Thus bowed low, they made themselves more vulnerable.

Another explanation links the knuckle with a knock and a practice once followed in arguments. Whoever was beaten admitted their defeat by knocking (knuckling) the underside of the table. In fact, in the seventeenth century to 'knock under' was still used in the sense of the modern to 'knuckle under'.

Some have seen the phrase as a description for a self-inflicted predicament. Totally drunk, people weakened in their knees so much that, no longer being able to stand upright or remain seated, helplessly they knuckled under the table.

LAGER BEER

LAY AN EGG

LEAVE NO STONE UNTURNED

LET DOWN ONE'S HAIR

LIFE IS NOT ALL BEER AND SKITTLES

LIKE A HOUSE ON FIRE

LIMOUSINE

LOOPHOLE

LUCKY BREAK

Lager beer

Lager beer is so called from the German word for 'storage' (*Lager*) because, to attain perfect quality, it was kept in a storehouse for a fixed period of time. It was first brewed in a Bavarian monastery in the fourteenth century.

Lay an egg

Oddly, used as a phrase, to 'lay an egg', points to a failure. Actors lay an egg when their performance falls flat, and likewise, comedians do so when their jokes fail to get a single laugh.

The expression, nevertheless, did not originate on the stage but in sport. A cricketer who scored no runs had a large zero placed next to his name on the scoreboard.

Spectators, always imaginative in their appraisal (and criticism), soon remarked on the resemblance of the shape of this 'nought' with that of an egg. So they called it a 'duck's egg'. Subsequently, they dropped the egg altogether, to keep the 'duck'.

Americans adopted the simile from the British, but adapted it to their way of life—both in sport and in food. Using it in baseball, they changed the duck into a goose, a fowl much more common in their country, portraying the zero in their figure of speech as a goose egg.

The French did not attribute the egg to any specific bird, but saw in the zero any kind of egg. Therefore for them—in tennis—a score of nil was just 'the egg', *l'oeuf*. When the English took over their way of scoring, they kept the (French) egg, which on their tongue sounded like—and eventually was spelled as—'love'. This kind of love signified nothing!

From the playing field, the figurative 'egg' spread to any walk of life where, slightly expanded, 'to lay an egg' came to mean a flop.

LEAVE NO STONE UNTURNED

To 'leave no stone unturned' is an advice going back well nigh two and a half millennia, to one of the early great battles fought in world history. It was given by the oracle of Delphi to Pausanias, the Spartan general in command of the allied Greek army in its decisive victory over the Persian forces at Plataea in 479 BC.

After defeating the Persians, Pausanias was determined to take possession of a treasure of gold, which, he had been informed, Mardonius, the enemy leader, prior to the encounter, had hidden somewhere on the battlefield. However, his efforts to locate what promised to be the most highly-prized booty failed. Not giving up the quest, he consulted the Delphic oracle. This directed him to 'leave no stone unturned'.

Thus, renewing his search, assiduously he explored every possible site, finally to discover the hoard of gold under the stones which covered the floor of the luxurious headquarters of the defeated Persian general.

Mostly historians study the events of the battle. But the counsel given at Delphi has lived on as a valuable admonition to everyone in pursuit of a worthwhile goal.

LET DOWN ONE'S HAIR

Throughout the ages, hair has served men and women in the most diverse ways, not least as a status symbol. It was a naturally-grown asset to beautify oneself and gain in standing of which both sexes made frequent use. They built up their hair into veritable pyramids, often further heightening themselves by elaborate, powdered wigs. Though these must have proved a burden, they nevertheless gladly carried it for the sake of appearance, attraction and social standing. It was all well worth the trouble.

Applying their demeanour to the style, it became very formal and assumed an air of ceremoniousness and solemnity. They must have felt relieved when at the end of the day or among their intimates, they could let go by 'letting down their hair'. The physical act survives in the metaphor.

Louis XIV of France, very conscious of his baldness, never permitted anyone to see the 'nakedness' of his head, for which reason his wig was his constant companion. He removed it only when retiring at night and, even then, did so himself, hidden behind the drawn curtains of his bed. From there, he handed it to a pageboy who was instructed to return the wig to him first thing next morning. How sad that a royal head was so restricted in letting down the hair, which was not even his.

Hair has been regarded as sexually attractive, if not arousing. Some religions, aware of the danger, make women cover their hair, if not all the time, at least so during a service, lest men's attention might stray from prayer. It was one of the original reasons for the custom, still adhered to by some congregations, for women to wear hats in church. On the other hand, in their portrayal of Mary Magdalen, traditionally a repentant sinful woman and former prostitute, artists show her with her hair hanging down to her feet.

To let down one's hair therefore also acquired a distinctly erotic note.

LIFE IS NOT ALL BEER AND SKITTLES

The English pub has always been an integral part of British life. A meeting place for the people, they gathered there to relax and enjoy themselves.

Innkeepers realised that the longer their guests stayed on

the premises, the more they would drink. At the time bowling, in the form of ninepins and known as skittles, was a favourite pastime. Wisely thus, the proprietors of public houses had bowling alleys and greens built adjacent to their establishments.

As an additional attraction, it greatly contributed to the happiness of the patrons and no less to the coffers of their host. 'Beer and skittles' came to express a lifestyle of delight and pleasure.

Sooner or later, however, people were to realise that life was 'not all beer and skittles'. The figure of speech was popularised by well-known poets and writers, and became so much a part of everyday language that it has outlived the game of ninepins which had played such a significant role in giving birth to it.

LIKE A HOUSE ON FIRE

Many of the early English homes, built of timber with thatched roofs, presented a great fire hazard. A spark from the open grate could easily set aflame the flimsy wooden dwelling and, in no time, reduce it to ashes.

An unforgettable traumatic experience, it has left its trace both in preventive legislation and in speech. It was responsible for the introduction of the curfew and created the phrase 'like a house on fire' as a metaphor for extraordinary speed and intensity, or for when two people get on very well with each other.

English villages are still admired for their thatched cottages, not realising the danger these once presented. American settlers putting up log cabins were equally exposed to high fire risks. Once aflame, little could be done to extinguish the conflagration which was so speedy that Americans, too, came to compare a fast horse as going like a house on fire. In America the phrase was popularised by Washington Irving's use of it in his 1809 humorous and satirical *History of New York*.

LIMOUSINE

A limousine is now a long, smart and luxurious car. But its origin was very mundane. Indeed, a type of peasant dress was responsible for the naming of the vehicle.

Limousin is an historic district in the centre of France and was, until the French Revolution, one of its provinces. Its inhabitants, but particularly the local shepherds, protected themselves against the vagaries of the weather by adopting a dress all of their own. A large hooded cloak, it almost completely enveloped them. It was so distinctive that people eventually identified it with the region. They called the coat after it—a limousin. The name soon spread far beyond.

When eighteenth-century carriage builders developed a new model of coach, reserved for the wealthy and pampered, they provided not only the passengers with a sheltered enclosure but by projecting the roof, equally protected the driver. Somehow it reminded people of the peaked hood so typical of Limousin and, in no time, they named the new model after it—a limousine. The name was retained, even when the horse-drawn coach was replaced by its motorised version.

Some doubt this derivation. They claim that it was not the roofed vehicle that first suggested its designation, but the driver who, by way of a uniform, used to wear a cloak reminiscent of the Limousin costume.

LOOPHOLE

People who try to circumvent the law without actually breaking it are always on the lookout for some subterfuge—a 'loophole'. For them it is a battle of wits and the term used for their subtle ploy is more appropriate than they could ever imagine. The loophole, originally, formed part of fortifications. It was a narrow slit in the walls, behind which archers took their stand. From there they could watch out for the approach of the enemy and were ready instantly to repel their attacks.

The opening was ingeniously constructed. Wider on the inside, it provided the archer with ample room to draw the bow. On the other hand, by becoming a mere slit on the outside, it gave extra protection against missiles fired by the foe.

Simple in itself, the loophole was a great advance in defensive warfare and is attributed to the Dutch. Loophole itself is derived from their language, from a root which spoke of someone 'watching' or 'looking slyly'.

LUCKY BREAK

To speak of a lucky break, at first thought, is self-explanatory. A long period of bad fortune which seemed never to cease is suddenly 'broken' by good news or long-delayed success. And yet the saying contains much more than the words suggest.

It recalls people's early fears when, haunted by superstition, they felt threatened by countless malevolent forces ready to do them harm. But they also believed that those fiendish demons were allergic to noise. Any sudden sound would drive them away. For this reason, the threatened individual would pick up any small stick or branch within reach and break it. The noise this made would have the desired effect. Literally, it was a 'lucky break'.

Some modern customs or habits are based on this early practice and assumption. It might well be the original reason for people snapping their fingers, cracking their knuckles or breaking a match in two. They might do so nowadays to release some inner tension. Apprehending an attack by evil spirits, they were convinced that they could scare them off by the noise they were making.

The solemnisation of a Jewish wedding concludes with the odd custom when the bridegroom breaks a glass by stamping on it. When hearing the sound, all those present call out 'good luck', its Hebrew rendering, *mazal tov*.

Psychologists know of many a case when people who experiencing good fortune or some newly gained happiness are afraid that it might not last, as envious forces will destroy it. To pay them off, they break some precious object!

Professor Sigmund Freud, who probed the recesses of the human mind, admitted that he himself was prone to such superstition. He gave a personal example. About to launch a treatise on one of his revolutionary ideas, to ensure its success, (as a sacrificial gift, as it were), he broke a valuable crystal vase. Indeed, a lucky break is part of the psycho-pathology of everyday life.

The phrase has also been associated with a game, and the world of entertainment. A pool player who succeeded in pocketing a ball on the first 'break' was lucky and could well speak of a 'lucky break'.

Travelling circuses—once the main attraction in an existence which still lacked movies, radio and television—very much depended on the weather. Rain, wind and snow would keep audiences away and their tents (and coffers) empty.

In their slang, circus people experiencing such a debacle would remark that 'it broke bad'. Nothing would be more welcome to them than a lucky break.

Magazine

That a magazine contains a great variety of articles is well justified by the very history of its name. Initially, this was the Arab description (*makhzan*) of a storehouse for grain and other cereals. It was then applied to buildings storing arms and ammunition. Crusaders picked up the word and idea while in the Holy Land, and introduced them in Europe. To start with, as 'magazine' it was exclusively employed for a place holding armaments. Its function was then expanded to become a warehouse for all kinds of goods. Its ultimate application in a literary sense—as a 'storehouse of information'—goes back to 1731.

In that year the first periodical appeared, known as *The Gentleman's Magazine*. It presented itself as 'A monthly collection to treasure up, as in a magazine, the most remarkable pieces on the subjects abovemention'd'. (It should be noted that the word 'pieces' at the time was the designation of the arms kept in the military magazine.) The novel sense of name caught on, and magazines of all types became an institution in the world of publications.

Maître d

Traditionally, many gastronomical terms are French, the language of a country renowned for its exquisite cuisine. Therefore it is only natural that the person supervising the menu of a restaurant is known as the maître d. Mysterious is the single letter in the title, but easily understood, when it is realised what it represents.

'D' was not the initial of the name of a famous cook. It is the mere shortening of the French *d'hôtel*. The *maître d'hôtel* is the 'master of the hotel', the head of the establishment or, more humbly, the chief steward.

MAKE THE GRADE

To achieve a goal necessitates some effort. 'To make the grade' applies to the achievement of a traveller who, having ascended a steep slope, has reached its top.

To make the grade had special significance in the early days of railway travel. Steep inclines needed extra power for the iron horse, the locomotive. For a steam engine to 'make the grade' was still a feat. Greatly admired, it served as an example for other walks of life which required exertion to surmount an obstacle in order to reach one's destination or pass a test.

To obtain a degree (or 'grade') at college or university is to *grad*uate. Those promoted in the armed services to a higher rank also have made the grade. In modern manufacturing the standardisation of products equally demands a quality that meets the (required) grade.

MANY A SLIP 'TWIXT THE CUP AND THE LIP

That there is 'many a slip 'twixt the cup and the lip' are well-known words, reminding people that nothing is ever certain till it is finalised. To rejoice in anything prematurely therefore is unwise. The axiom is based on a classical legend associated with the Greek Ankaios. Famous as a skilled navigator, after Tiphys' death he became helmsman of the *Argos*.

While in the process of planting a vineyard, he was approached by a slave who, solemnly addressing Ankaios, foretold that he would not live to drink of its wine. Soon after his sinister prophecy, a miracle occurred. The saplings just planted instantly produced grapes which immediately ripened. To prove the slave wrong in his ominous prediction,

Ankaios lost no time in having some of the grapes taken to his home to press their juice into a cup.

However, at the very moment he was about to drink from it, with the soothsayer slave still present, a messenger arrived. He carried the bad news that a wild boar had destroyed the vineyard. Devastated, Ankaios forgot all about drinking the wine to rush off in pursuit of the animal. Though he caught up with the boar, he did not succeed in slaying it. Instead, it killed him.

Thus, Ankaios was never able to enjoy the wine. It proved the veracity of the observation that there is 'many a slip 'twixt the cup and the lip'.

MARATHON

A marathon now generally refers to a contest of endurance, a task extending over some considerable distance or time, needing great stamina. The name recalls the site of one of the many battles fought between the Persians and the Greeks during the first half of the fifth pre-Christian century. The Persian forces were advancing victoriously towards the west, conquering one country after another. In 490 BC in the Plain of Marathon they were confronted by the Greek army which, under the command of Miltiades, counted just over 10 000 soldiers. It was outnumbered three times by the Persians.

In desperate need of more men, the general dispatched Pheidippides, the fastest runner among his soldiers, to Sparta, to ask for reinforcements. Pheidippides covered the vast distance (amounting to 240 kilometres (150 miles)) in two days. But it was an abortive mission. Assistance was refused. Religious reasons, he was told, made it impossible for members of the Spartan army to be dispatched prior to the next full moon—much too late to be of any help.

Undaunted, and without the aid of an ally, the Greeks thus

joined in battle. In spite of their numerical disadvantage, they defeated the Persian army overwhelmingly. Once again, Pheidippides was sent off, this time to Athens (42 kilometres (26 miles) away) to announce the victory. His second 'run', too, was essential. It was feared that the Persian fleet, still unbeaten, might attack the city. With the lack of communication, the men defending Athens might prematurely surrender if unaware of their countrymen's triumph at Marathon. Once aware, they would be all the more determined to resist any invasion, holding out till backed up by the returning victorious fighters.

No doubt already fatigued by his previous race to far-off Sparta and back, Pheidippides reached his destination totally exhausted. With his last breath he reported the victory. Gasping, 'Rejoice—we conquered', he collapsed and died.

His run became historic. Now no longer part of military operations, it is re-enacted as a foot-race. As a significant sporting event, it was included in 1896 in the then revived Olympic Games. On the occasion, to the gratification of everyone, it was won by a Greek peasant.

Forgotten now are the martial circumstances of the first marathon and its tragic ending.

The race became standardised to extend over a distance of 42 kilometres (26 miles).

Marathon originally was the name of the fennel plant. No doubt it grew abundantly on the battlefield and hence gave it its name. Of pungent smell and yellow colour, it served as a favourite flavouring in Greek cooking. Roman gladiators used it as an early additive to food, in the belief of its efficacy as a stimulant. Even the wreaths used to crown victorious gladiators were made of the plant, the marathon.

MARCHING ORDERS—LEFT FOOT FIRST

To start something on the right foot is not only an expression, but a custom once almost obsessively observed. To get out of bed 'on the wrong side', and enter a home with the left foot first, augured misfortune. A notable exception is the marching of soldiers. They are trained to step out with their left foot first, and well known is the marching order 'left, right, left, right'!

The shouted command 'left, right' may roll off a sergeant major's tongue more easily and smoothly than 'right, left'. But there is another explanation for putting your left foot first, and it is based upon superstition.

The majority of people are right-handed. Consequently, their left is their weaker side. Superstitiously, they believed that evil forces, out to do them harm, cleverly would attack them from the left. This 'left' came to be identified with the devil, which explains why the Latin for 'left' became the English word 'sinister'.

It is no wonder then that putting one's left foot first was seen as an indication of evil and of aggressive intentions. To enter a home thus showed hostility. One of the original functions of footmen which also explains their name was to guard the entrance of a home to watch visitors' feet and make sure that they would not enter with their 'hostile' foot first. It followed that, in contrast, an army, trained to be aggressive, would start marching with their left feet first. Magically, it was imagined, this would increase their fighting prowess. Most of all, they would gain the assistance of all the dark and sinister forces of the occult world. A vivid illustration of this choice of foot in military action is an early frieze, excavated at the Mausoleum in Bodrum, Turkey. It shows a soldier engaged in 'hand to hand' (!) combat, kicking his enemy in the groin with his left foot!

This background may well be the primary (though now forgotten) reason for the martial tradition of giving priority to the left foot. Even if no occult power came to the soldiers' assistance, the very practice would psych them up to be at their most aggressive.

MARE'S NEST

A mare's nest points to a most disappointing experience. Believing to have made a significant discovery, it turns out to be an illusion and worthless. Horses do not build nests and therefore to find such is not possible.

A typical example of such an abstruse occasion is the story of a seventeenth-century English astronomer. Watching the skies through his telescope, he astonished the world by the sensational news that he had discovered an elephant on the moon. The announcement turned out to be completely unfounded. What he had really seen was a little mouse, which had found its way inside the telescope and had got stuck between the lenses. Greatly magnified, it had misled the star gazer to believe it to be a pachyderm.

MARZIPAN

A confectionery similar to marzipan most likely was already known in Roman times as an offering to the gods. Folklore, however, gives the credit of its invention and naming to the German city of Luebeck. Its citizens claimed that the confectionery was first made—literally—within its walls and that, therefore, the credit should go to their town. The sweet confectionery, in fact, was the outcome of a bitter war.

During a prolonged siege, Luebeck's granaries were empty and food was getting scarce in the city. All that was left in its stores was an odd variety of goods: almonds, oil of roses and sugar. It was obvious that unless some nourishing provision was quickly obtained, the population was bound to be starved into surrender. This prompted the city council to offer a reward to anyone who could find some way to combine the odd assortment of ingredients still available, and create some wholesome food which could sustain the people.

Ingeniously a baker was able to produce out of the leftovers the desired fare which—apart from being nutritious—proved a delicious confection! He distributed the first batch on the feast day of St Mark. In search of a name for his concoction, he appropriately called it after the saint, 'the bread of St Mark', *Marci Panis*. Fused into one (word) it became marzipan!

MASTERPIECE

The description of a work of outstanding value, particularly in the field of art, as a masterpiece, goes back to English goldsmiths and their guild and their pursuit of perfection.

No one was admitted to their craft until he had proved that he could master it. To do so, an apprentice had to submit to the guild a piece of art he had completed without outside assistance. Appropriately it was referred to as his 'masterpiece'. Representatives of the guild carefully and critically examined it. If they agreed that it came up to the high standard set by them, the apprentice was invited to join. Taking the oath of loyalty, he became a fully qualified member of the craft, a 'master of arts'.

MICKEY FINN

A Mickey Finn refers to some drops or a substance surreptitiously added to the food or (mostly alcoholic) drink of an unsuspecting person as a fast-acting laxative or knock-out. It may be meant as a mere joke but also has a serious, if not sinister purpose. Originally, a Mickey Finn was not intended for human consumption but, in the form of a pill or powder, was administered to animals, particularly horses, as an evacuant.

The name has been associated with a variety of people. Some say 'Mickey' was a barman who introduced the practice to rid his premises of patrons who, having indulged in too much liquor, proved troublesome. Suffering almost instant diarrhoea, they made a hurried exit.

The second Mickey Finn was a Chicago gangster. He was renowned for his conjuring tricks and specifically his sleight of hand. It was not difficult for him, working behind the bar, unobtrusively to slip a strong knock-out into the drink of whomever he had chosen as his victim. The moment he was unconscious, Mickey robbed him.

Opinions vary as to the nature of this fast-acting and effective 'knock-out'. Some believe that the additive was a hypnotic or barbiturate. Others identified the substance with chloral hydrate.

MISSIONARY POSITION

The practice during coitus for the woman to lie on her back with the man on top of her is known as the 'missionary position'. It is a bewildering and weird description indeed. And yet its explanation is part of the history of religion and Christianity's effort to convert pagans.

When missionaries first visited the Polynesian islands, they were shocked by many native customs, not least by those related to sex. The people's unusual manner of intercourse seemed particularly sinful to them. They thus taught their charges to adopt the only position they regarded as proper, moral and permitted by God. Simultaneously, it would enable them to fulfil the command ordained by God for woman always to be below the man!

The Polynesians duly discarded their old ways of intercourse which they now considered sinful and followed the new practice 'religiously'. In acknowledgment of their clergymen-teachers, they called it the 'missionary position', a name easily misunderstood or misinterpreted, but retained ever since.

MOB

Originally, an unruly and excited crowd was referred to in Latin as *mobile vulgus*, 'the moveable public.' 'Moveable' was used in the sense of their excitability, being fickle and disorderly. Easily, they would change their attachment and support from one side to the other.

Through the years, the term was abbreviated, first so in the seventeenth century. After initially omitting its 'public' (vulgus) part, even the remaining *mobile* section was cut short, to leave 'mob'. Strange to observe that of the expression only its 'everchanging' portion was left.

From the 1930s onward the term 'the mob' was used in the United States for members of the underworld, eventually specifically the Mafia.

MOLLYCODDLE

To pamper and dote on a person is to 'mollycoddle' them. It is a combination of words which, as it were, put the cart before the horse. It really speaks of coddling a molly. To coddle was once used for looking after an invalid and—according to one derivation—to feed them spiced hot drinks or a thin gruel. Molly has been traced back to the Latin *mollis* for 'soft'. It was a pet name for Mary, at one time given specifically to milkmaids, as well as to feeble, effeminate men. To refer to people being mollycoddled thus contemptuously spoke of their being truly spoiled and overindulged.

MONKEY WRENCH

Among the various tools fulfilling the function of a spanner is the monkey wrench. Many believe that its intriguing name was suggested by its adjustable jaws. They reminded people of a monkey chewing its food. It has also been thought that the tool was so easy to handle when tightening nuts that even a monkey could do it.

Alternately, it was asserted that the implement was called after its inventor, a Mr Monk or Moncke. If so, his identity has never been definitely established. Some say that he was an English blacksmith. Others give the credit to an American mechanic who in the 1850s worked for a firm in Massachusetts. At first people acknowledged the creator of the tool by referring to it as a Monk or Moncke wrench. But as the name meant very little to them, soon, perhaps out of mere fun, they came to call it a monkey wrench.

It would be a strange reversal of the Darwinian theory. He taught that man had descended from the ape. In the case of (the name of) the monkey wrench, it would be the other way round: a man was its ancestor.

MOONLIGHTING

Moonlight has played a significant role in a variety of circumstances. It has been seen as the source of a person's sleeplessness and being unsettled mentally, particularly when the moon is full.

'Moonlighting' acquired a sense all of its own. It was concerned with activities pursued when the sun had set. The much weaker moonlight cast a shroud over what was happening and made it difficult to identify individuals.

A typical example of such 'moonlighting' was the hunting by poachers during the night.

Towards the end of the nineteenth century, the term was applied specifically to the exploits of patriotic Irishmen who, during the hours of darkness and in disguise, raided the homesteads of English landlords who had evicted impecunious Irish tenants from their lodgings. They frequently sent a warning note prior to the raid, which they signed 'Captain Moonlight'.

Eventually, the early meanings and associations of moonlighting were forgotten, for the term came to acquire a much more harmless connotation. Moonlighting now spoke of people who, though paid to do one job, unbeknown to their employer or the taxation authorities, earned extra money, doing so after hours.

MOONSHINE

Moonshine, similar to moonlighting, refers to things done or obtained during the hours of darkness. In England, it became the name of brandy smuggled from France into the country by night to evade the payment of excise. In the United States, both during the days of prohibition and also to avoid government taxes, people made their own whiskey by night—

in their private stills. Appropriately, they spoke of their illicit produce as 'moonshine'.

MORTARBOARD

Mystifying indeed is the customary name of the academic cap 'mortarboard'. No less intriguing is its peculiar shape. Both are closely interrelated.

The mortarboard developed out of a special type of skull cap. Covered with a loose square of material, the combination proved most impracticable. Frequently the cloth flapped into the wearers' faces, obstructing their view and altogether being a nuisance. To remedy this, the cloth was replaced by a stiff square board covered with black fabric and firmly attached to the skull cap.

The new contraption reminded people of the board used by construction workers, which, loaded with mortar, they carried on their heads. They called the new headcovering a mortarboard, nominally transferring a tool of the building trade into the field of education!

An alternate derivation discovers in the mortarboard remnants of a cap once donned by French kings and judicial dignitaries. Its outlines strikingly resemble those of an upturned mortar (the French *mortier*), the cup-shaped bowl used to pulverise drugs and other like substances with a pestle.

MUCKRAKING

Heads of state and politicians have left their mark in many ways. President Theodore Roosevelt has the distinction that, apart from making valuable contributions to his own country, he gave the English-speaking world a new word—'muckraking'.

He first used it in a dinner speech to the Washington Gridiron Club, on 14 April 1906, in which he discussed the writers who had set themselves the task to expose corruption in public places. An essential mission, they could pursue it responsibly and with the welfare of the nation in mind. However, there was also the danger of sensation-mongers who for the sake of publicity and to create a scandal, besmirched innocent people's names by making unsubstantiated charges. Roosevelt admitted that 'the men with the muck-rake are often indispensable to the well-being of society'. He qualified his statement by adding, 'but only if they know when to stop raking the muck'.

His muckraking metaphor soon caught people's imagination. It gained wide currency and became part of the vocabulary. Roosevelt had not invented the word but, as he himself explained, merely adapted it from John Bunyan's *The Pilgrim's Progress* (first published in 1678). In this popular allegory of a dream, Bunyan portrayed the encounter with a peculiar sort of man. He could look no way but downwards and had a muck-rake in his hands. With it, he 'raked to himself the straws, the small sticks, and dust of the floor', all the filth.

MUG SHOT

A mug shot is generally associated with photographs taken by the police for the identification of suspects or criminals.

The term owes its existence to drinking mugs. Made of ceramic, they used to portray faces, usually with distorted features. A ruffian's mien often reminded people of those grotesque mugs.

There is also a suggestion that the 'mug' literally means a 'face'. From the Sanskrit root *mukha*, gypsies had adopted the word in India and, after adapting it to their tongue, brought it to the western world.

Mum's the word

'Mum's the word' is said to people if they are expected to keep what is being told them strictly secret. It has nothing to do with one's mum.

It has been thought that mum is all that is left of *mumbling*. Those who mumble cannot be understood. Anything confided to them almost inevitably remains undisclosed.

More feasible is a physiological explanation. To produce the 'm' sound, the lips have to be compressed. Consequently, when one 'm' follows another, the mouth remains shut. Trying to duplicate the 'm', nothing is said. In the attempt to voice the inexpressible—'mum's the word'.

As with many other everyday phrases, here, too, credit must be given—at least for its popularisation—to Shakespeare. In *Henry* VI (Part II), one of his characters counsels, 'Seal up your lips, and give no words but mum.'

NAKED TRUTH

Cynics may find special significance in the fact that 'the naked truth' is the product of a fable!

Told in ancient Rome and related in the works of Horace, it spoke of both 'Truth' and 'Falsehood' going for a swim. Taking off their clothes, they jumped into the river.

They did not stay together for long. Falsehood got out of the water first. Stealing Truth's garments, she dressed in them, leaving hers behind. When, eventually, Truth left the river and discovered that her clothes were missing, she refused to don those of Falsehood. She preferred to remain naked and go forth into the world as the 'naked truth'.

NARCOTICS

The name of 'narcotics' goes back to Greek mythology and is linked with the figure of Narcissus. A youth of extraordinary beauty, he was passionately loved by the nymph Echo. But he did not return her feelings and, in fact, ignored her approaches. This hurt her deeply. In spite of the rebuff, she could not forget him. She pined away till, finally, nothing was left of her, except her voice, her echo!

In punishment, the gods caused Narcissus to suffer an even more cruel fate. They made him fall in love with his own reflection in the water. It was a futile yearning and, doomed from the outset, bound to end in tragedy. One day, Narcissus, enamoured with his image in a pool, leaned over too far, fell into the water and drowned. After his passing, the gods changed his body into a flower, now called after him, Narcissus. Properties contained in some of its species, can produce numbness and sleep. Drugs derived from them, recognising their source, bear the name of narcotics.

Nepotism

What modern colloquialism calls 'jobs for the boys' is not a new phenomenon. Already, centuries ago, there were people in authority who, when making appointments to lucrative positions, gave preference to members of their family without regard to seniority, ability or qualifications. That their favouritism became known as nepotism reflected their close relationship to those chosen to hold office. The term is derived from the Italian for 'nephew' (*nepote*), a designation once also used generally for close relatives.

The coinage of the term goes back to Pope Alexander VI, notorious for his abuse of power. After his elevation to the papal throne in 1492, he distributed the most influential ecclesiastical offices to his nephews and other members of his family. One of his nephews, for instance, was appointed cardinal, while he made Cesare, his own son, then a mere youth of 16 (and born to him by a Roman lady prior to his assuming the papal office), archbishop.

It did not take long to secularise the abuse and for it to become a common, unfortunate feature in almost every walk of life, practised by people who lack integrity in positions of power.

Nest egg

A nest egg is money kept in reserve for times of need. Now a mere figure of speech, originally it referred to the custom of placing an artificial (china) egg into the nest of a hen believing that this would encourage the bird to lay a real one next to it.

NICK OF TIME

Making a notch or nick into a stick of wood known as a tally was an early method to keep account of money owed or lent.

Notches in sticks are said to have served also to record time, with each nick representing a specific hour. A person arriving at the very last moment could be said to have come 'in the nick of time'. The practice and idiom was adopted as well in the scoring at matches. If a goal was shot at the very end of the game, justifiably people said that it was scored just 'in the nick of time'.

NIGHTCAP

In the northern climate, nights at times are freezing. With rooms unheated, to protect their heads against the cold men used to cover them with a cloth cap which, appropriately, they called their 'nightcap'.

Times changed. Bedrooms were no longer icy. But men retained the nightcap—with a significant difference. They applied its name to the hot, and preferably alcoholic, drink (the 'toddy') they imbibed prior to retiring, to warm their insides.

NINE DAYS' WONDER

As one of the disappointments of life, success and fame are short-lived. That they have been described as a nine days' wonder has been explained in several ways.

After birth, kittens and puppies are blind for approximately nine days, during which, as it were, they live in a world of wonder. Once their eyes are opened, everything becomes very ordinary. Humans, likewise, may be deluded for a certain period of time. However, as in the case of the young cat or dog, eventually their eyes are opened, their illusion ends and they have to face reality.

The figure nine has been a mystical number of great potency, being three times the trinity. Therefore it was believed that the true facts became apparent after exactly nine days.

In the Roman Catholic faith, the devotion known as the *novena*, as its Latin name indicates, extends over nine days. Once completed, it might immediately be followed by another one. Of identical length, its object totally replaces that of the preceding nine days of prayer which, having been relegated to the past, is almost entirely forgotten.

Likewise, religious festivals of the church once were kept for nine days. During this time the image of a saint in whose honour it was celebrated was carried round in procession. Centuries earlier, in pagan times, the ancient Romans recognised in terrifying storms an omen of forthcoming disaster and were convinced that by keeping a period of nine days of supplications they could prevent its occurrence.

It is quite possible that the religious institution and tradition, once well-known and widely practised, was adopted as a metaphor and applied to earthly matters which, at the time when they happened, seemed sensational. They, too, were limited and, after nine days of glory their appeal would vanish, with the event soon sinking into oblivion.

Nit picking

Those who look out for and (delight in) minor errors and faults are said to be nit picking. Originally, this was not a mere metaphor. It referred to the unpleasant task of removing the small eggs of lice which stuck to people's skull and hair.

It seems that those fussy pedants who make it their

business to point out and pay attention to the smallest and least significant detail, often besmirching others' actions or ways of life, take special pleasure in their dirty work and merit being called nit pickers.

NITWIT

Whoever speaks of a nitwit, unknowingly and unintentionally, recalls an early antagonism of the English for the Dutch. To call anyone a nitwit made fun of the genuine Netherlander who, if ignorant of a subject, freely admitted it by saying 'I don't know', which in Dutch is *Ik niet wiet*. The 'nitwit' mimicked this sincere remark.

OCCAM'S RAZOR

OFF THE CUFF

ONE-NIGHT STAND

OSTRACISED

Occam's razor

Little is known about the personal life of William of Occam (or Ockham), the 'Doctor invincibilis'. Born in 1300, he died on 10 April, though in which year is not certain. It might have been in 1349 or 50, when the Black Death was raging in Europe. An outspoken English philosopher, he clashed with Pope John XXII and was excommunicated. Subsequently imprisoned, he succeeded in escaping, to spend the rest of his life in Munich, where a street is still called after him.

Challenging the mind, he wrote his political works in the form of philosophical disputations. He presented all the arguments for and against, leaving the conclusion to the reader.

Occam now is best (and possibly solely) known by the maxim 'Occam's razor'. Called after him, actually the phrase does not appear anywhere in his writings. It is based on his teaching and conviction that one should always concentrate on the essential and avoid any unnecessary digression: 'Entities must not unnecessarily multiply'.

Occam himself assiduously applied the principle, dissecting every problem as with a razor and eliminating—cutting off—superfluities.

Off the cuff

That impromptu speeches are said to be made 'off the cuff' once had a good reason. After-dinner speakers used to jot down on their cuffs any idea that came to them during the meal, which they could then include in their address. Very literally, thus, they entertained the guests 'off the cuff'.

Much more likely, the phrase goes back to the time when cuffs, apart from being decorative, were found useful in another way. Around the 1900s, waiters' cuffs, made of celluloid, were detachable. Much more quickly soiled than the shirt, they could be removed to be washed separately. It was also realised that instead of chalking up orders on slates, which was the custom then, waiters could note them down on their cuffs so much more easily. Once they had served the food and the bill was settled, the cuffs could be wiped clean again.

Hollywood film directors have been given credit as well to have led the world in all that is done 'off the cuff'. It often happened that while they were watching a movie being shot, new ideas came to their minds which, they imagined, could improve the script. Not to forget them, they quickly scribbled them on to their cuffs...

Cuffs are no longer a detachable item on men's shirts nor (ab)used as note pads of a kind. Nevertheless, remarks are made and audiences addressed 'off the cuff'. The alternate description of the practice as speaking *ex tempore* was first used by Cicero, the second-century Roman statesman and philosopher renowned as an orator.

ONE-NIGHT STAND

New lifestyles may completely change the meaning of well-known phrases and expressions, a fate experienced by the 'one-night stand'.

In modern promiscuous society the term is taken unambiguously to refer to people having casual—one night—sex with an almost total stranger. Originally, the one-night stand had no erotic connotation. It was part of actors' lives. Travelling theatrical companies went from place to place. To cover vast areas of territory and to ensure a full house on each occasion, they restricted their performance to a single night. Theirs was a 'one-night stand'.

Ostracised

Anyone ostracised is shunned by society. The term used is significant not only in its etymology but as part of history. It goes back to the ancient Greeks and their concern for the preservation of democracy.

If a political leader became too powerful or, by his dictatorial manner, was thought to threaten the people's freedom, a majority vote of citizens could remove him—at least temporarily—from his office and the country.

The way this was done took the form of a referendum which necessitated a minimum of 6000 votes. These were registered by means of earthenware tiles or potsherds cast into the ballot box. They were known as *ostrakon*, a Greek word derived from the description of an oyster shell. No doubt they were so called because they resembled it.

Citizens who felt that the accusation was unfounded left their *ostrakon* blank. Those agreeing with the indictment, inscribed it with the would-be dictator's name—they 'ostracised' him!

No trial was held and no evidence required. Neither could the accused defend himself. Within ten days during which time he was given a chance to wind up his personal affairs, he had to leave the country. The maximum period of banishment was ten years, later reduced to five. He was not deprived of his personal property or civic rights, both of which he resumed on his eventual return.

The institution of ostracism was one of the significant reforms introduced by the Athenian statesman Cleisthenes on his assuming office in 508 BC and first applied 20 years later. It was abolished only towards the end of the fifth pre-Christian century by Alcibiades, who himself had been one of its victims.

Archaeologists have unearthed almost 1000 *ostrakons*, with the still legibly-inscribed names of politicians exiled in classical times.

PAINT THE TOWN RED

PARASITE

PEDIGREE

PENKNIFE

PENTHOUSE

PERSON

PHONY

PICKET

PIGEONHOLE

PIZZA

PLAY DUCKS AND DRAKES

PLAY SECOND FIDDLE

POKER

POKER FACE

POOR AS A CHURCH MOUSE

PORK BARRELLING

POTHOLES

PRIVATE EYE

PULL OUT ALL THE STOPS

PUNK

PUT ON THE SPOT

PAINT THE TOWN RED

People who, in uninhibited exuberance, go on a spree are said to 'paint the town red'. A colourful description, it has given rise to several possible explanations, ranging from the innocuous to the violent.

An early meaning of to 'paint' was to 'drink'. Those who imbibed an excess of liquor were thought to show their overindulgence by a red complexion, if not of their faces, at least their nose. Intoxicated, people might lose self-control. Giving vent to their feelings, they would light fires which, with their red glow, lit up the city's streets.

It has become the custom for brothels, bars and (often illegal) gambling places to be aggregated in one specific neighbourhood, well-known to those in search of them. It is not uncommon for groups of sailors or other men, jointly on the loose, to go on a drunken spree. Their obvious choice of destination is that part of the city known as the 'red light district'. Its colour, as it were, rubbed off on them and their revelry. 'To paint the town red' has become a euphemism for their notorious visits to this disreputable part of town.

As fire and blood are red, the colour became symbolic of danger and of violence. It is no wonder, therefore, that the high jinks of inebriates frequently generate hooliganism and, with its ensuing bloodshed, leaves its traces on the pavement. It is a real but regretful way of painting the town red!

American Indians, too, have been credited with the introduction of the phrase. When still on the warpath, after having sacked a town, they often would set it on fire. And did not the flames that shot up into the sky paint the town red?

PARASITE

A parasite lives at the expense of its host. It is a sponger. All the word innocuously says—in Greek—is 'beside food'. That was the parasite's original 'position' in early Greek religious cults. As the representative of those making an offering, the parasite actively participated in the ritual and, in acknowledgment, shared the priests' food, and as a further gift, received a portion of the sacrifice.

It was a rewarding occupation and a welcome opportunity to live at other people's expense. Greek dramatists soon took hold of the idea and gave the parasite a place of its own, now totally detached from religion. They made it a stock figure of comedy—who gatecrashed parties, flattered the host and, in any argument, however undeserved and unjustified, took the host's side. Even the name given in some farces indicated the parasite's special role. There was 'Mr Soup', for instance, so called as he always turned up at the very beginning of a meal, not to miss even its first course.

From the sanctuary and the stage, the parasite then was adopted in the nomenclature of nature, to become as well the description of a creature or plant that lived at the expense of others. It took everything from its host without giving anything in return.

PEDIGREE

Genealogists tracing a family's ancestors used to indicate the descent of each individual member by a small arrow. In their eyes, the sign very much resembled the 'foot of a crane'. This made them call it so, in French, *pied de grue*. Run together and Anglicised, it created the 'pedigree' which was then applied to the entire graph of the family, with its numerous crane feet spread all across.

Suggestions that the pedigree actually relates to the 'degree' of relationship, though factually true, have no etymological significance.

Applied to the animal world and disregarding its avian connection, the pedigree became a valued documentation of descent and pure breeding.

PENKNIFE

Throughout the Middle Ages and until the nineteenth century, the quill served as a major writing tool. It explains why the very meaning of 'pen', derived from the Latin *penna*, is 'feather'! Mostly, this was obtained from the wings of geese, crows, turkeys or even peacocks.

That pocketknives are called penknives is an anachronism and yet a fitting reminder of progress. It recalls the time when people used quills for writing. Constant usage blunted the feather's point, which needed sharpening. Always to be ready for such an eventuality, scribes carried small knives in their pockets, identified by their purpose as 'penknives'.

PENTHOUSE

Those who live in a penthouse may not realise that the description of their residence shares its main part with the (useless) appendix. Both names are derived from the same Latin root used for something 'attached'. Their mere position thus was responsible for the choice of their name. The appendix is 'attached' to the intestines, the penthouse to the very top of a block of flats or apartments.

PERSON

In the fight for complete equality of women and against man's dominance, in all walks of life, including speech and writing, the use of the genderless 'person' has assumed a new significant role. It hides the gender behind a mask—and does so quite literally.

The first 'person' appeared on the classical Greek and Roman stage. The actor did not show their real face, but covered it with a mask. It was not to camouflage their identity, but to fulfil a dual function. By the very mask worn, the actor indicated to the audience the type of play they were about to watch and their part in it. There were two kinds of masks: a laughing face and one expressing sadness. From their first appearance thus, the actor told by their coun-tenance whether their role was a happy or a tragic one.

The mask had an additional advantage. With no modern electronic aids, actors, to be heard, depended solely on their voice. A cleverly constructed mask amplified the volume of the spoken word, acting as a megaphone. The mask therefore not only reflected the character portrayed, but made it so much easier for those taking part to make themselves heard 'through the sound', which in Latin is *per sona*. It is the source of the present-day 'person', sexless and, paradoxically now, so impersonal.

PHONY

Anything fake is 'phony'. It is no wonder therefore that the term describing something counterfeit first gained currency in the early 1900s in the American underworld.

Its etymology is uncertain and explanations proffered have been decried as phony as well. No specific data supports the theory that it is merely a cut-down (tele)phone, which conveys sound alone without any further substance.

Phony has also been quoted as the corrupted name of a one-time manufacturer of inferior jewellery, sold at a high price—a Mr Forney.

Another suggestion discovered a close link between the expression and people's fawning. Both shared the elements of being unreal and deceitful, which made the fawning attitude lead to all that is phony.

As something fraudulent, phony may well recall, in a corrupted form, which would be most suitable in its case, the 'fawney ring'. It was once used in English slang for a worth-less ring, palmed off as a valuable object to an unsuspecting customer. Swindlers conned buyers by switching a solid gold ring for a fake one, a practice which became known as 'fawney dropping'.

Phony was really 'funny', it was also said. Therefore it was well suited to be applied to any kind of funny business, especially if the joke was on the other person.

Finally, as a word expressing scorn and contempt, it was thought, phony really stood for 'phooey'!

PICKET

Pickets play a prominent role in modern industrial action by stopping would-be strikebreakers from entering the premises. However, they are not as recent as may be assumed. In fact, the first picketing by unionists took place in England around the 1860s.

A militant action, its description actually is of military origin. Armies posted a soldier or a small detachment as 'pickets'. They were to watch out for the enemy and give early warning of its approach.

The name of the picket goes back to the French, *piquet*. Sharp-pointed stakes or pegs were so called. They served a variety of purposes. To start with, horses were tied to pickets.

They were also used in the construction of palisades, built around army camps. By mere association, the soldiers patrolling this protective fence, or placed there as guards, were called after these pickets which gave birth to the word in its modern sense. The stakes also survive in the picket fence that divides or marks the boundary of modern homes.

PIGEONHOLE

Pigeons have made their distinct contributions to daily life. They have left their traces both on buildings and in speech. In either case, they did so in a negative, if not destructive way. Their mark on structures certainly has had a corroding influence. In matters that needed attention, they gave their name to prolonged delay, if not oblivion.

The divisions embodied in roller-top desks or bureaus look very much like the pigeonholes of a dovecote, specially provided for the nesting of the birds.

To start with, to pigeonhole a matter, such as a letter, a document or an application, solely referred to filing them, putting them into their proper compartment. Unfortunately, language, as do customs, often deteriorates. This was exactly the fate of the concept of pigeonholing. Once papers had been filed away for future reference, they were forgotten. The matter they dealt with was not just deferred, but lost sight of altogether. It was as if the pigeons had flown away.

PIZZA

Pizza pies are Italian. Their description has nothing to do with their actual content, although one hypothesis discovers in the pizza, slightly deformed, the medieval Greek word for a 'cake', which is *pitta*. Much more likely is the suggestion that, not referring to anything edible, the pizza recalls a simple tool. It was named in Old Italian after its 'sharp point', *pizza*, probably derived from *pizzicare*, to 'prick'. Italian bakers used it to decorate the edge of the pie by pressing the tool into the soft dough.

An apocryphal story traces the pizza to Naples. It tells how necessity was the mother of its invention. A Neapolitan baker had run short of dough to prepare the traditional pie, and did not have enough left for its upper crust. Ingeniously, he lined the tin with dough which, before baking it, he topped with chopped meat, cheese, anchovies, olives and such like.

Unexpectedly, the end result proved so delicious that soon people clamoured for the novel pie. All that remained for him to do was to give his creation a name. What better choice than that of the very gadget he had used for it. So he called it a pizza, which it has remained to the present day.

Some culinary experts have denied the Italian source. They assert that, in reality, the idea of the pizza comes from Armenia whose people used to top a bread-like crust with minced lamb.

PLAY DUCKS AND DRAKES

Whoever plays ducks and drakes with their money spends it carelessly. They throw it away just for the pleasure of seeing it go. This made people compare the short-lived enjoyment with the old simple pastime which became a favourite children's game known as 'ducks and drakes'. All it required was a flat stone. They threw it across the water of a pond to watch it skimming over its surface. To the imaginative eye the skipping stone looked like 'ducks and drakes' taking off from the water, which explains the choice of name for the game.

No matter how forceful the toss, eventually the stone lost its impetus, ultimately to sink to the bottom. The joy given by playing 'ducks and drakes', indeed, was limited, just as the enjoyment of money by those who squander it. To describe such irresponsible wastage by the name of the game was all the more appropriate, as frequently people used coins instead of stones which, after their short passage across the water, were irretrievably lost.

PLAY SECOND FIDDLE

There is no hidden meaning in the metaphor that speaks of someone playing second fiddle. It says exactly what it means.

The second violinist in an orchestra obviously plays a less important role than the first violinist. As it were, the violinist comes only second in every sense of the words. And so it is in any walk of life.

POKER

The origin and meaning of poker is as uncertain as the outcome of the game. Though most likely it originated in Europe, where the first literary mention of poker goes back to the sixteenth century, it was developed and became a favourite card game as late as the nineteenth century in the United States.

It has been linked with a similar German card game in which bluffing and betting played a significant part. This was known in German as *Pochspiel*, from *pochen*, a word literally meaning to 'knock' or to 'rap', but also used metaphorically for 'boasting' and 'bragging'. Germans are supposed to have called the game so because a player, when passing, used to say *ich poche*, simultaneously doing just that—knocking on the table with their knuckles.

When, in New Orleans, the French adopted the game, they could not produce the German guttural sound (its 'ch' being voiced like that of the Scottish 'loch'). Instead, they pronounced the *poche* as poqué (poe-kay) which then further deteriorated into the American poker. If not bluffing, it certainly is confusing.

Another explanation derives poker from the French *poche* for a 'bag', the very word which gave English the 'pocket' and the 'pouch'. The name of poker therefore referred to its all-important and so coveted kitty or pool, containing the money.

There is also a Dutch claim, in which language the devil was known as *pokker*. At the very time the game became a favourite gamblers' pursuit in the United States, *pokerish* was the vernacular for anything 'frightening' or 'alarming'. And was not indeed the novel pursuit devilishly frightening? Hence, to call it 'poker' seemed most fitting.

POKER FACE

It seems so obvious that the making of a poker face, showing no expression, goes back to the game in which 'bluffing' one's opponent plays such an important role. By keeping a straight face, the player does not give away their 'hand', particularly essential if the combination of cards they hold would make them lose the game.

And yet, there is also a theory which claims that the origin of the phrase is not connected with the actual game. It might have been 'forged', as it were, in the fireplace. The poker used to stoke the embers in the grate is a metal rod. Its very rigidity permits no change of shape or appearance. A poker-face, equally unbending, betrays no emotion and, by controlling every facial muscle, conceals one's true attitude and feelings.

POOR AS A CHURCH MOUSE

Once, a church, as a spiritual centre, provided no food. Consequently, it had no cupboards or pantry, as might nowadays be the case, with social functions often being held on the premises as well. This made a mouse living in a church poor indeed. It could not find even a crumb of bread.

The original English proverb, stemming from the seventeenth century, and the source of the present-day phrase, much more aptly did not refer to anyone as 'poor' but as 'hungry' as a church mouse.

PORK BARRELLING

Though 'pork barrelling' is a coinage of American politics, it has made its way across the seas to other English-speaking countries.

The phrase describes the practice of members of the House of Representatives to have federal treasury allocate special funds for projects favoured by (and of benefit to) their constituency. The pursuit certainly gained (and retained) them votes among their electorate.

The term is said to have been adopted from the Deep South, where it had particular significance in antebellum (pre-Civil War) days. Though often refuted, this tradition claims that plantation owners occasionally used to treat their slaves with a gift of salted pork. Delivered in huge containers, their arrival created a veritable stampede among the blacks. Each one tried to get to the barrel first to get hold of as much of the meat as was possible.

However plausible the derivation sounds, it has been rejected as a mere fable. Pork, it was said, was easily available to the slaves at the time. More likely, it has been suggested, the 'pork barrel' of modern political manoeuvres merely enlisted the use of 'pork' as a common slang term for corruption and graft. Already congressional records of 1879 had spoken of St Louis receiving some of the 'pork'. What they really meant was the 'fat' of the land, with which to buy patronage.

POTHOLES

Potholes in roads, of every size and depth, add to traffic hazards. Nowadays, they are mostly caused by the number and size of heavy vehicles, bad weather or lack of maintenance. Their mystifying description however, points to an origin of a possibly totally different kind.

Potters, it has been said, in need of clay for their wares, did not go to far away places to obtain it. They just dug it up from a road nearby, 'producing' the original potter's hole which, if not in size, in name, contracted into the modern 'pothole'.

PRIVATE EYE

For a detective to be known as a private eye has been seen as the result of the shortening of his profession's description as that of a Private Investigator, using the latter word merely for its initial. Properly rendered thus, he therefore ought to be spelled 'Private I'. However, the principal credit for the adoption of the designation must go to Allan Pinkerton. He was the American Sherlock Holmes. Yet, while Sherlock Holmes was a figure of fiction, Pinkerton was a real man. A Scot by birth, he pioneered detective work in the United States. His life story is an epic.

Born in 1819, in the slums of Glasgow, he was the son of a warder at the local prison. Because of his father's death, he had to leave school as a child of eight. Forced to earn a living at so young an age, he served an apprenticeship as a cooper.

Pinkerton became involved in local politics. As a fervent Chartist, he took up the fight for the rights of workers. Threatened with arrest, he fled the country in 1842 to migrate to the United States. Settling at Dundee, Illinois, he made his living as a barrel-maker. Fate then caused a change in career. Discovering a counterfeiting ring, he realised his special gift for detecting crime. After serving as a sheriff and succeeding in the capture of several criminals, he was appointed as the first (and then the only) detective of the Chicago police force.

Of alert mind and initiative, he saw his opportunity to establish his own private National Detective Agency in the city, in 1850. Soon the name of Pinkerton became a byword in crime detection, not least so because of his flair for public relations. Astutely, he chose a wide-open eye as the logo of his agency, with 'We Never Sleep' as its slogan.

Pinkerton gained national prominence due to his many enterprises and assignments. They included missions for the American secret service, the solving of widespread robberies and guarding Abraham Lincoln on his trip to Washington for his inauguration as president.

The name of Pinkerton became synonymous with crime detection and people came to refer to his firm as the 'Eye'. It was through the writings of Raymond Chandler, most of all, that the 'Private Eye', based on Pinkerton's logo, assumed its present-day connotation.

PULL OUT ALL THE STOPS

Anyone pulling out all stops goes all out to achieve an objective, withholding none of the resources at their disposal.

The phrase comes from playing the organ. The instrument was known already in pre-Christian times, though churches adopted it only as late as the fifth century and then, to start with, in Spain alone. Eventually, organ music was recognised as adding to the beauty of a service. With one exception. Puritans resented and rejected it. To them it was mechanisation of worship, and they nicknamed the instrument 'a chest of whistles'. In expressing their contempt, they chose one of its main features: the many pipes with their diversity of sizes.

The great variety of sounds the pipes produced was achieved by means of air (or 'wind') pumped into them through special holes (or 'mouths'). The number of whistles used was controlled by wooden slides. The way these were positioned either activated the pipes or stopped them from making any sound. The latter function was responsible for their being called 'stoppers', often shortened to 'stops'.

The organist pulled out the particular stopper (singly or in combination) necessary to give the item rendered the tone and volume desired.

Organs greatly varied in the number of these stops. This could range from a few dozen to many hundreds. Pulling out all the stops used the organ to its fullest capacity and, inevitably, resulted in the maximum volume of sound of which the organ was capable. There was no holding back.

PUNK

The modern punk has quite a past. Once, anything punk was regarded as of little use or value. A punk therefore was a worthless sort of person, a good-for-nothing.

Sixteenth-century Britain applied the name to a prostitute or any obliging female who, enjoyable in bed, was praised as 'a punchable wench'. According to one view, the word—very suggestively—was derived from the slang for 'sperm'.

In New England, USA, anything smelling foul was referred to as 'punk'. American Indian speech used the word for decayed wood. When burnt, it emitted a nauseating stench.

After a period of disuse in the 1880s, the term experienced a revival in the United States, becoming the designation of the hobo, and as the result of a strange combination of circumstances. Handouts given to tramps were mostly chunks of dry bread. As these looked and even smelled very much like decayed wood, they resurrected, as it were, the earlier punk. Its new application was reinforced by the odd coincidence that bread in French is *pain*, in sound so reminiscent of punk. All this added up to the hobos being identified with the bread they were given, and to be called punks. Soon their name was linked with thugs and, eventually, in the slang of criminals, with homosexuals.

In modern times, punk became popularised through the American author Dashiell Hammett, the writer of detective and mystery fiction, who applied the term to offenders distinguished by out-of-the-way sexual practices. In its new sense, punk gained worldwide currency through the Bogart movie *The Maltese Falcon*.

The punk then became a social phenomenon. In the late 1970s, idle unemployed teenagers in Britain, resenting the indifference shown to their plight by the general community, were determined to demonstrate their protest and to do so most conspicuously and by flouting traditional values. In pursuit of their aim, they adopted what they called the 'punk look'. Each of its features cried out for attention. No one could ignore their unconventional dress, their brightly dyed and stiffly lacquered hair, and their general appearance of repulsive neglect. Nor could anyone close their ears to their deafening, raucous music.

Their ultimate goal was both to express and to create anger, fear and pity. Indeed, the outsized safety pins they frequently sported on the clothes they wore were meant to symbolise their helplessness. The punk was not a rebel only, but as vulnerable as a baby in nappies!

Extraordinary is the history of the punk. It leads from the early harlot to a figure of despair in twentieth-century society.

PUT ON THE SPOT

To make suspects tell the truth, those in authority used all kinds of methods. At times, these were most inhumane, violent and cruel. They included torture, the successive pulling of teeth till none was left, and depriving a person of food and drink for days on end. The catalogue of inquisition is a sad record of ordeals.

It took some time before the force of public opinion stopped the abuse and the guardians of the law were made to apply more humane ways for their interrogations. One of them particularly was of an odd nature. A small square chalk mark was made on the floor. The suspect was then compelled to stand 'on the spot'. He was not allowed to move from it till he had made a full confession or had satisfied those questioning him that he was not lying. The process, often extending over many hours, was intended ultimately to prove beyond endurance, so that the person 'on the spot' broke down and confessed. Unfortunately, this included even the innocent who, just to end the ordeal, admitted to crimes they had not committed!

No wonder that the trial, by being 'put on the spot' too, in the end was abandoned, and few people would ever know that it existed. Nevertheless, it has left its traces in everyday speech as a phrase now applied in much less fearsome and frightening conditions. People who find themselves placed in some awkward predicament are 'put on the spot'.

Totally different circumstances have also been quoted as a source of the saying, associating it with death threats! Those out to kill a person sent him the ace of spades, a card with one black symbol at the centre, long regarded as an omen of death. Whoever received it could not mistake the message and, well realising the seriousness of his position, had every reason to be scared. It could truly be said of him that he was put on the spot and wisely should take notice of the warning.

QUI VIVE
QT

Qui Vive

Alert people are said to be on the *'qui vive'*. They are watchful and keep a sharp lookout. Though their attitude is not typically French, the phrase is unadulterated—Anglicised neither in pronunciation nor spelling.

It received its present-day meaning from the early use of the phrase. Originally, it was a (French) sentry's challenge to anyone approaching, equivalent to the English 'Who goes there?'. During hostilities, the soldier on guard wanted to know on whose side the visitor was, and who they supported. Literally the words said 'Who lives?'. This might well be a shortened form of 'Long live who?'. A loyal subject was expected to identify his allegiance by replying *'Vive le roi'*—(long) live the king.

QT

QT are truly puzzling characters, like a mystic formula. Anyone saying or doing things on the 'QT' does so 'off the record', if not surreptitiously, and expects the other party to keep 'quiet' on the matter. It is this very silence that the QT represents, using solely the initial and final letter of *quiet*. That, traditionally, these are spelled with capitals merely emphasises the importance of secrecy.

RACK ONE'S BRAINS

RACKETEER

RAVIOLI AND VERMICELLI

READ BETWEEN THE LINES

RED AND WHITE FLOWERS

REGATTA

RHUBARB

RIDE PIGGYBACK

RIDE ROUGHSHOD OVER SOMEONE

RIGHT AND LEFT IN POLITICS

RING TRUE

RINGS A BELL

RITZY

ROMAN HOLIDAYS

ROSELLA

RUB UP THE WRONG WAY

RACK ONE'S BRAINS

Trying very hard to recollect something temporarily forgotten or to find the solution to a problem, one 'racks one's brains'.

Dramatically, the portrayal of the effort makes figurative use of the rack (from the German *Reck*). A most cruel instrument of torture, it was once employed to make people confess or submit, against their better judgement and beliefs.

Gruesome indeed was the function of this infernal gadget. The person interrogated was tied by their hands and feet on to a frame or sort of ladder. This then was gradually extended, to 'stretch' (*recken* in German) the body. It was hoped that the pain caused by the ensuing dislocation of joints and the body literally being torn apart, would make the victim 'remember'—'rack the brain'. They would supply their torturers with the desired information and thereby, as they termed it, help them to 'find out the truth'.

It is interesting to note that the equivalent German idiom speaks of 'breaking one's head'.

RACKETEER

Racketeers cleverly now mostly make their gain 'on the quiet'. They seem far removed from the early days and ways which gave them their name. This recalls the 'racket', in the sense of noise, profiteers used to create whilst engaged in their pursuits.

What form the racket took has been explained variously. Unconvincing is the suggestion that it was the loud noise crooked gamblers made when throwing their (loaded) dice. The designation has also been traced to the practice of gangsters who, unable to obtain 'contributions' quietly, persuaded their victims to hand over money by loud threats and the sound of their guns.

Another origin of the 'noisy' name links it with a practice of petty thieves. To distract the attention of their intended victims, they let off crackers in the streets or caused some other racket which created confusion. This made people look round to see what had happened. It was the opportune moment for the crooks to pick pockets.

It has also been alleged that American gangsters were the first racketeers. They arranged alleged charity functions to which they invited the very wealthy. Those who turned up as honoured guests found that they had been duped. In a rowdy gathering (the 'racket'), they were forced to donate large sums to their hosts.

In the end, the original 'noise' became identified with the shady business and gave the racketeer as a silent partner in crime its present-day meaning.

RAVIOLI AND VERMICELLI

A variety of factors have suggested the names given to food. They included its distinctive flavour or smell, the place where it was first grown, created or eaten. A no less significant role was played by its appearance, which accounts for why ravioli and vermicelli were so called.

Small pockets of pasta stuffed with minced meat or cheese, they resemble miniature turnips. Turnip in Italian is *rava*. Though so totally different in taste and ingredients, its very shape prompted Italians to call the pasta after (the diminutive of) the vegetable—*ravioli*.

Vermicelli, on the other hand, might not be too appetising to finicky eaters if they realised that this kind of pasta received its name because it looks like 'little worms'— *vermicelli* in Italian.

READ BETWEEN THE LINES

Generally, it is expected that people mean what they say and say what they mean. But on occasion, there is a hidden meaning in their words as well, and those astute enough can 'read [it] between the lines'.

Now used (mostly) metaphorically for guessing inferred information, to start with the phrase was taken very literally. Conspirators and secret agents inserted their message 'between the lines' of a letter they had written. They did so with invisible ink.

Codes were used from early times, for example by Julius Caesar in some of his battle reports. Their employment was intended to prevent important information falling into the hands of foes or of a competitor. Personal and private notes could thus equally be assured of secrecy—unless (and until) cryptographers were able to break the code.

One of the most famous messages conveyed 'between the lines' (though not literally in this case) was responsible for the foiling of the gunpowder plot in 1606. When Francis Tresham got to know of the planned blowing up of the British Houses of Parliament, he was most anxious to save the life of his brother-in-law, Lord Monteagle, who was sure to be present in the Upper House on the occasion. But it was impossible to communicate directly with him and inform him of the threat. Indeed, he did so in an apparently innocuous letter in which—unnoticeably for the ordinary reader—he inserted the urgent advice for him to stay away because of the 'terrible blow' about to be struck. His message was contained (and hidden away) in alternate lines! The Lord must have been well acquainted with the method of cryptographic writing which in this historic instance led to the discovery and frustration of the conspiracy.

Red and white flowers

A widespread English superstition, also adopted elsewhere, regards it as unlucky to bring a bunch of mixed red and white flowers to a patient in a hospital.

The superstition is based on an ancient belief in floral magic. Red and white flowers, it assumed, by their very colours, would trigger off supernatural forces, causing the recipient to bleed to death (the result of the red), ultimately thus taking on the (white) pallor of a corpse.

One tradition links the superstition specifically with the Crimean war. Wounded soldiers then believed in the harmful magic potency of flowers of those hues. They would make them bleed profusely and, consequently, necessitate lots of white bandages.

Regatta

A regatta, as a sport and a term, is the legacy of Venetian gondoliers to the world. The Italian description of 'a struggle for mastery' and a friendly 'strife', it was first applied by seventeenth-century gondoliers, when racing for supremacy along the Grand Canal. Traditionally, they called their contest a 'regatta'. Their choice of name had a good reason. *Regatta* is the diminutive of the Latin *regus* for 'a royal head'. And Venice was ruled by a doge—a 'little king'. As the race was run in his honour and for his entertainment, it was only right in its designation to pay tribute to his position.

RHUBARB

Revealing is the story of rhubarb—both as a plant and as a slang word.

Rhubarb came to the western world twice over. In antiquity the Greeks imported it from what is now Russian territory, where it grew in abundance around the Volga river, then still known as Rha. Its very source, it was thought, was responsible for its name, first given it by the Greeks, who called it *rha-barbaros*. The word itself has been explained as either being the original, pre-Slav description of a 'root' or a shortened version of a Greek recollection that it had been imported from the *barbarian* country of the river Rha.

Barbarians to them, of course, were all foreign people, whose language they could not understand. For this, they did not blame their own lack of knowledge but genuinely assumed that the mere reason for their not comprehending what they said was that these aliens suffered from a speech impediment. They were like 'stammerers', for which the Greek word is *barberos*, still thus surviving in the rhubarb as in the barbarian.

The second country of origin was China. Between the fifteenth and nineteenth centuries, the roots were exported from there via the Levant to Europe. It was believed that eating rhubarb improved one's state of health, as it resulted in 'pouring' excess humours from the body. Shakespeare makes mention of rhubarb in this very sense in Macbeth.

People have often wondered how the 'h' found its way into rhubarb. It might well be—figuratively speaking—an overflow from the river Rha. Some scholars, though, have associated it with the Greek *rhein*, for to 'flow', possibly still a reminder of its original source, the flowing river which was to become the Volga. Adopted in England, the plant's Greek name was shortened to rhubarb.

That to Americans 'rhubarb' served as a slang word for a

quarrel, a noisy argument and a fracas, particularly so on the baseball field, may go back to the stage. To make a mob scene appear real, imitating the sound of an angry and hostile crowd, actors or stagehands repeated the word 'rhubarb' again and again. By doing so, they created the desired illusion.

Ride piggyback

To ride piggyback has nothing to do with being transported by means of a pig. It is the result of the slurring of words and the well-known experience that people are apt, unthinkingly, to adopt and perpetuate mistakes once made. The original phrase, which can be traced back to the sixteenth century, spoke of pick-a-back and referred to the pitching of a load—a pack—on one's back or shoulders.

Ride roughshod over someone

In early times of combat, still unmechanised, the horse was enlisted to help man in fighting his wars. He used it not merely as a means of transport or a mount, but as an actual 'live' weapon. Brutally, it was ridden over the bodies of fallen enemies to crush them to death. To make the manoeuvre all the more effective and deadly, the horse was roughly shod. The sharp nails of the shoes purposely left protruding added to the severity of the injuries inflicted on the prostrate foe.

The cruel practice has left its mark in the idiom that speaks of those who treat others harshly, without paying regard to their feelings, as 'riding roughshod' over them.

The spiked nails on the horses' shoes proved of value in

peacetime as well—in the field of transport. During the winter, when the roads were covered with ice and snow, a horse could easily slip and throw the rider. To prevent such mishaps, blacksmiths shod them roughly. The nails left sticking out enabled the animal to get a better foothold.

RIGHT AND LEFT IN POLITICS

The differentiation in politics between the 'right' and the 'left' and their identification with conservatism and socialism respectively, goes back to the last days of the French monarchy. Though now part of political terminology everywhere, it does not really tie in with the British parliamentary system or any other system derived from it. The term, so emotive now, once reflected merely a seating arrangement.

In the British parliament and therefore the Westminster system, it is the tradition for the members of the ruling party to occupy the benches on the right side of the Speaker's chair. In consequence, representatives of the opposition sit on the left. They do so irrespective of their political affiliation. As a result, when a socialist government rules, it is on the 'right', its conservative opposition on the 'left'. The apparent paradox perpetuates a memorable occasion, not of British but of French history.

In 1789, the French monarchy was fighting for its survival. In a last attempt to save it, the king tried to show his willingness to listen to the people. He convened an advisory body, something that had not happened for almost 200 years. It embodied the representatives of the various classes into which the community was then split. The allocation of their seats was almost a foregone conclusion and reflected the mores, divisions and attitudes of the time.

Traditionally, those of superior standing and to be shown

respect occupied the right-hand side. (At a banquet, for instance, or any formal gathering, the host always invited an honoured guest to be seated on the right.) In the circumstances, it was also the 'rightful' place for the nobility. Inevitably, the delegates of the 'common' people, known as 'the third estate', had to take their seat on the side still unoccupied which, of course, was the left. Simultaneously (and then very obviously) their placement indicated their inferior status. The position in front of the president of the assembly soon was identified with certain political views, resulting (and maintained to this day) in the meaning of the 'right' and the 'left'.

The underpriviledged, still fighting for equality, obviously, were regarded as radicals, whilst the nobility and aristocracy, anxious to retain their privileges, of necessity were 'conservative'.

Even the reference to the left and right 'wing' of a party had a meaningful beginning. 'Wing' was a military term, used in battle. Applied in politics, it reflected the frequent militancy of members in propounding and fighting for their views.

RING TRUE

Anything that rings true can be trusted. It has no fault. It is like the clear ringing of a bell that has no cracks. Not church bells, however, but coins were responsible for the phrase. To test whether they were genuine and not counterfeit, they were dropped and, to the experienced ear, the sound they made indicated that they were not fake.

Rings a bell

Something that jogs the memory 'rings a bell'. It is like suddenly remembering from childhood days the sounding of the school bell and all it meant at the time.

The expression recalls how, through the ages, a bell was rung as a reminder and a call to action. It indicated imminent danger or told members of a congregation that a service was about to commence.

Differently, in the United States, the phrase refers to the gaining of an object, eagerly desired and pursued. If the bell rings, one's efforts have proved effective. The figure of speech used in this sense, might well have been suggested by the bells rung in shooting galleries and amusement parks, whenever someone hits the bull's eye or successfully completes a difficult task, winning a prize. In its modern version, it is like the bell ringing when a lucky player has 'pulled' the jackpot of a gaming machine, the 'pokie'.

Ritzy

By his perfectionism, Swiss-born César Ritz not only enriched the hotel industry but the vocabulary. His name, in the form of *ritzy*, became synonymous with anything that was elegant and luxurious or, if overdone, flashy and pretentious. Ritz was born in Niederwald in 1850, the thirteenth child of an Alpine shepherd. Migrating to France, he accepted any job that offered itself. This included feeding elephants in the Paris zoo. He liked to say that it was his first step in the catering trade.

In 1898, he opened a hotel in the French capital. From the outset he was determined to make it the best of its kind in the world. For this purpose, he engaged as its chef Escoffier, then recognised as a master of cuisine and unsurpassed in the art of cooking.

Not only in the food, but in every sphere Ritz aimed at providing his guests with the best. He himself slept in each room, to make sure that all the beds were comfortable.

His efforts paid off. Having succeeded in Paris, he moved to England to carry on what he had started on the Continent.

In 1902 he suffered a nervous breakdown from which he never recovered. He lived as an invalid for sixteen years. In spite of it, he made the plan for his second great venture, the Ritz Hotel in London. He was present at its opening in 1905, but was never able himself to manage it. Nevertheless, it bore his name and, as he had wished, offered the ultimate in service and luxury. New York soon followed. And thus his name and fame spread worldwide, spelling out elegance, splendour and sumptuousness.

Ritz died in Küssnacht, Switzerland, in 1918. But his name has survived these many years by being adopted by the finest establishments, even more so, in being recalled whenever anything is referred to as 'ritzy'.

ROMAN HOLIDAYS

Throughout history governments and rulers who faced grave problems—often of their own making—have cunningly tried to divert the minds of the people. They did so by providing them with special 'treats'; and entertaining them with spectacular celebrations. In the words of the Roman poet Juvenal, they gave the people 'bread and circuses'.

Worse still, they would organise what became known as a 'Roman holiday'. This catered for the sadistic streak in people who gained special pleasure from watching others suffer. To keep the loyalty of their subjects, the ancient Roman emperors staged barbaric spectacles in public arenas in which gladiators, facing insuperable odds, were doomed to meet a cruel death.

The phrase was coined by Lord Byron, who first used it in his famous poem *Childe Harold*. It portrays a captured Gaul who, forced to fight as a gladiator, was 'Butcher'd to make a Roman holiday'.

ROSELLA

Early settlers in Australia had the exciting experience of encountering creatures unknown to them so far. Many a story is linked to the names they chose for them.

It was around Parramatta in New South Wales that they first saw a beautiful, multicoloured parrot. At the time, Parramatta was still known as Rose Hill. It was named in honour of George Rose, the then secretary to the British treasury. Initially his name had been given to the house built for Governor Phillip. It was then transferred to the entire district, for which it was used from 1788 to 1791.

The name bestowed on the bird underwent several changes. To start with, people simply linked it with the bird's apparent habitat. They called it the Rose Hill Parrot. Dropping the parrot, it became known as the Rose Hiller. Finally, slurring the words and no longer realising their local significance, they contracted the Rose Hiller into the rosella, by which name the parrot has been identified ever since. Its description carries with it part of early Australian history.

RUB UP THE WRONG WAY

To 'rub someone up the wrong way' certainly has nothing to do with a massage. The figure of speech used for upsetting a person by words or actions they resent may well be derived from the observation of an animal's reaction to what humans do to it. If a cat's fur is stroked the wrong way, it will not only look scruffy, but feel discomfort and disconcerted, and will not hold back from expressing its displeasure by voice or claw.

On the other hand, the phrase may have been first coined in connection with inanimate objects. If 'rubbed up the wrong way', they will show the traces of such inappropriate, and possibly damaging, treatment. A carpet of fabric, for instance, rubbed (or in modern times vacuumed) against the pile, looks untidy.

The expression may even go back to the Elizabethan era with its spacious homes. These had oak floorboards, which had to be carefully looked after. If servants mopped or rubbed them against the grain, they became streaky and unsightly. 'Rubbed up the wrong way', they aroused the anger of the lady of the house.

SALMONELLA
SAME VEIN
SANDWICH
SCAB
SCHNITZEL
SEE NAPLES AND DIE
SENT TO COVENTRY
SEVEN-YEAR ITCH
SEVEN YEARS' BAD LUCK WHEN BREAKING A MIRROR
SHERRY
SHOTGUN WEDDING
SIAMESE TWINS
SILHOUETTE
666, THE NUMBER OF THE BEAST
SKELETON IN THE CUPBOARD
SKULL AND CROSSBONES
SLAPSTICK
SLIPSHOD
SLOGAN
SLUSH FUND
SNOB
SOLSTICE
SOW WILD OATS
SPEAKEASY
SPICK AND SPAN
SPILL THE BEANS
SPINSTER
SPITTING IMAGE
SQUARE
STADIUM
STAG PARTY
STARK NAKED
STEPMOTHER AND STEPFATHER
STIFF UPPER LIP
STONY BROKE
STRAW THAT BROKE THE CAMEL'S BACK
STRIKE WHILE THE IRON IS HOT
STUMBLING BLOCK
STUMPED
SUCKER
SWEEPSTAKE
SYCOPHANT

Salmonella

Among the most feared and virulent food poisonings is that caused by salmonella. The 'salmon' contained in its description is misleading and does not refer to the fish. Its name honours Daniel Elmer Salmon (1850–1914), an American veterinarian and one-time chief of the Bureau of Animal Industry, who inaugurated systematic meat inspection and a quarantine period for imported livestock. He was the first to identify the bacteria responsible for the contamination.

Same vein

'In the same vein' refers to something of like kind. However, it is not a blood-related term, as might be imagined. It belongs to mining operations and, metaphorically speaking, has been dug up out of the earth. Minerals, ore or coal of similar type are confined to specific layers underground. They can be found 'in the same vein'.

Sandwich

Everyone eats sandwiches. Few realise however that the first of its kind was prepared for a member of the nobility, whose very name it perpetuates. He was John Montagu, the fourth Earl of Sandwich (1718–92). A notorious gambler, at times, without respite, he would spend an entire day and night at the card table. So possessed by the game, he would not even take off a few moments for a hurried meal. That is why on one such occasion (c. 1762), he instructed his servant to bring him a thick slice of beef stuck between two pieces of bread. This impromptu snack he could easily eat without interrupting his gambling.

His improvisation of a meal did not go unobserved, and soon began to catch people's imagination. They adopted the earl's idea and, in acknowledgment, called the repast after him, a sandwich.

Actually, the practice of serving food in the form of a sandwich antedates John Montagu by more than 1800 years. It goes back to the ancient Romans. The Jews adopted it from them and continue annually to recall and re-enact the custom by a religious ceremony. During the Passover meal, taken on the eve of the festival, they partake of a special kind of sandwich. The tradition is explained in the prayer book used on that night. It tells that 'this was the practice of Hillel', the most outstanding rabbinical authority of the first pre-Christian century. He used to combine the unleavened bread and the bitter herbs and ate them together, no doubt in the way of a (Roman) sandwich.

SCAB

There are at least three suggestions why a member of a union who refuses to join in industrial action, working while his mates are on strike, is despisingly called a scab. The worker is compared with scabies, the obnoxious skin infection. Slightly less pejorative is the explanation that this portrayal as scab applies the term used for the crust forming on sores which it is always a pleasure to remove...

In the scab has also been discovered a Latin root, which would make the worker a 'shabby' person, a loathsome 'scoundrel'.

SCHNITZEL

Taking the meaning of *schnitzel* literally, it would be an exceptionally thin and small slice of meat. From the German, its name is derived from the carving of wood chips, known as *schnitzen*. It is an odd association which makes the choice of its name even more surprising. The *schnitzel* is expected to be tender and not to remind those eating it of a piece of wood.

SEE NAPLES AND DIE

The superb beauty of Naples has been regarded as so overwhelming that, once having seen it, no other place could ever equal it. To visit any other city would be an anticlimax. This, it is generally believed, originated the adage 'see Naples and die'. Having experienced its splendour, there is nothing left to enjoy.

However understandable the praise, it appears odd. After all, the recollection of beauty makes it all the more precious and enriches life. Therefore there is another suggestion which recognises in the saying a warning to visitors. At one time, typhoid and cholera were rampant in Naples and those who had come to enjoy its sights easily fell victim to the scourges.

Many a pleasure-seeking visitor contracted venereal disease, which equally abounded in the city as a busy seaport. With antibiotics still non-existent, the infection took its toll and, quite literally, those who had come to see Naples subsequently died. It justified and made sense of the saying.

SENT TO COVENTRY

Countless visitors now go to Coventry, the famous English cathedral city, which also was the home of 'Peeping Tom'. At one time, however, 'to be sent to Coventry' was a disgrace and a punishment, responsible for the present-day phrase. Those who are 'sent to Coventry', are ostracised and cold-shouldered. No one will associate with them.

Two explanations have been proffered for the origin and meaning of the saying. At one time, it is asserted, the citizens of the city were strongly anti-militarist. They would not have any contact with the soldiers of the local garrison. A girl seen to fraternise or merely talk with any of its men was instantly shunned.

Among the worst disciplinary measures meted out to members of the army deserving punishment thus was 'to be sent to Coventry'. The hostile treatment given to soldiers there became known nationwide. It resulted in the phrase 'to be sent to Coventry' eventually being applied generally, to anyone tabooed.

Others have linked the saying with the English Civil War in the seventeenth century. In this historic confrontation between King Charles I and parliament, Coventry was strongly anti-royalist. Supporters of the king who had been taken prisoner and found troublesome in Birmingham, were therefore sent to this Cromwellian stronghold. In Coventry they would find no friend, and be treated with disdain. Totally isolated, it was tantamount to being in solitary confinement.

SEVEN-YEAR ITCH

The popular idea of a 'seven-year' itch', when spouses seem to be tempted to have extramarital affairs, can be traced to the belief that a personality change occurs every seventh year.

Less convincing is the 'diagnosis' which associated the alleged phenomenon with a troublesome irritation it took seven years to clear up.

Seven years' bad luck when breaking a mirror

The superstition that the breaking of a mirror would result in seven years of bad luck is related to a myth.

It was believed that a mirror magically absorbed a person's very essence. Therefore whoever broke a mirror destroyed part of themselves. It was further assumed that it would take seven years to repair the damage done and to restore the individual's shattered wholeness.

This specific period of time was not haphazardly chosen. Seven was a sacred number, ever since Babylonian and Assyrian days. As there were seven planets in the heavens, worshipped as divine, so everything in the cosmos moved in cycles of seven. Roman anatomists thus imagined that it took the human body seven years to renew itself, which they accepted as an anatomical fact. Once the damage had been done, with its subsequent bad luck, this could not be eliminated until seven years had elapsed, the period necessary for the human body to regain complete good health, vigour and good fortune.

Sherry

It has taken a long time for sherry to become what it is today. The name of this Spanish product would confuse even the most sober. It has no relationship to the beverage itself which was originally a still white wine. Experiencing many a metamorphosis, it perpetuates the city in whose region it was first cultivated, situated 120 kilometres (75 miles) south of modern Seville and near to Cadiz.

Established as a Roman settlement in honour of Julius Caesar, it was called *urbs Caesaris*, the 'city of Caesar' or, in brief, Caesarea. When the Moors occupied the town, they did not change its name, but in their accent it sounded totally different. Caesarea became Sheres. History so willed it that it was located just on the frontier of the Moorish kingdom. Christian Spaniards to the north thus referred to it, in their tongue, as *Xeres de la Frontera*, 'Xeres on the border'. When, in 1264, Alfonso X conquered the Moorish territory, and with it the city, he retained its name. But since it was no longer a border town, Alfonso X rightly dropped its 'frontier', whilst rendering its remaining part as 'Jerez'.

The English, taking a great liking to the drink, imported it to their country. In the process, however, they misinterpreted its historic, geographical name. To their ears the Spanish pronunciation of the former Arab name which had replaced the Latin one, sounded very much like *Heb-reys*. They mistook its final 's' for the English plural. Pronouncing the name as sherries, they erroneously imagined therefore that as a single drink it would be 'sherry'. That is how, by mere mistake, the modern aperitif came into existence.

It is an intriguing tale of a drink, which reflects the changes of history and the effect of errors produced by a confusion of tongues. Whoever would suspect the presence of Julius Caesar in every sherry?

SHOTGUN WEDDING

In former days, for a girl to give birth to an illegitimate child used to stigmatise the entire family. Therefore, a man who had made a girl pregnant was honour-bound to marry her. Because he often did so only at the very last moment possibly is one reason why the enforced solemnisation of the marriage is called a 'shotgun wedding'. It is 'celebrated' in a hurry and under duress.

More dramatic is another interpretation of the explosive terminology. A man not willing to do 'the right thing' by the girl was made to do so by her concerned father, anxious to protect his daughter's reputation. At the nuptials, he stood by with a shotgun at the ready, just in case the reluctant bridegroom and father-to-be might try to make a getaway at the last moment. It was indeed—and very realistically so—a shotgun marriage.

SIAMESE TWINS

To compare an indissoluble attachment with that of Siamese twins, oddly and regrettably goes back to sensational displays of freaks of nature. It was coined in the United States to promote sideshows exploiting the unfortunate fate of two brothers.

Born in Siam, present-day Thailand, in 1811, Chang and Eng were twins, the sons of a Chinese father and a mother who was half-Chinese and half-Thai. They were born joined by a ligament at their breastbones.

Sadly, in more senses than one, jointly they grew up, and engaged in the poultry business till, dramatically, their lives changed. While on a visit to Bangkok, a merchant discovered them. He immediately realised their commercial value and persuaded their mother to let him take care(!) of them. He took Chang and Eng, then 18 years old, to Boston. From there they were made to tour the whole of the United States. Exhibited as freaks of nature by P.T. Barnum in his circus, they were billed as 'the Siamese Twins'. And it was this advertisement which coined the term!

Becoming naturalised American citizens, they adopted the name of Bunker. In 1846, they married two sisters, sleeping in a bed for four. They were to father 22 children, of whom 20 were born normal and two deaf mutes.

Their fame and publicity did not make Chang and Eng happy. Though twins, they were totally different in character. They often quarrelled. There were personal problems they had to face. While one brother was a teetotaller, the other became an alcoholic. For long periods of time, they did not speak to each other, which made them truly silent partners. Oddest of all was their decision to have separate homes, in reality an impossibility and a problem solved by living in each alternately. No doubt, they must have been the most peculiar foursome that has ever existed.

On 17 January 1874, at the age of 63, the brothers died within three hours of each other. Their sad fate has become history, hardly remembered by anyone. But, paradoxically and abstrusely, the expression 'Siamese twins', born out of their misfortune (and its commercialisation), has become synonymous with the closest possible friendship.

Chang and Eng were not the original Siamese twins, though the first to be so called. The earliest record of twins of their kind anticipates them by some 700 years. It goes back to the twelfth century to the English village of Biddenden, Kent, which makes their name even more paradoxical. The first known Siamese twins thus were not indigenously Thai, but British! Eliza and Mary Chulkhurst, born c. 1100, were joined at their shoulders and hips. When at the age of 35 one of the twins died, her sister was advised that, to save her own life, the dead body had to be surgically removed from her side. She refused. Together they had come into this world, she said, and together they would depart. Within six hours, she joined her sister in death.

The 'Biddenden Maids', by which name they became known, are remembered annually in their village by a special dole distributed among the poor, and cakes baked in the twins' honour carrying the impression of their figures.

SILHOUETTE

Not infrequently, an appointment as treasurer or minister of finance has not been an easy one. Their task of balancing a nation's budget, often implied the imposition of increased or additional taxes. A Frenchman filling the office in the eighteenth century experienced this very fate. Almost paradoxically, it gained him world renown and caused him—without his wish—to make a personal contribution to art and the vocabulary of all nations.

Étienne de Silhouette was the French minister of finance, known as 'controller-general' [of the economy], for just over eight months in 1759. During this short period, he greatly antagonised the people by the introduction of measures which considerably reduced their living standards. New levies raised by him included a special poll tax on bachelors and a consumption tax. On the other hand, he cut government pensions. His ensuing unpopularity, in fact, led to his premature resignation.

To express their dislike of the man who had lowered their lifestyle and wealth so much and, simultaneously, to ridicule him people used his very name as a byword for niggardliness and diminution of substance. They referred to it as being 'according to Silhouette' (*à la Silhouette*). New expressions, now and then, experience a strange fate. It was the case with this phrase coined to voice disaffection. Just at that time, it had become fashionable to replace, or at least supplement, expensive portraits painted in oil by shadow drawings. Comparatively inexpensive, they showed merely the outline of the figure. They seemed as parsimonious as the treasurer. What better way than to call them silhouettes?

On the other hand, it has been suggested that those pictures were so designated because making them was one of Silhouette's hobbies. Another theory claims that though he himself did not create them, he liked them so much that he owned a large number, which he displayed both in his office and his castle. This made visitors soon call them by his name.

Cynically, it has also been said that the name of the silhouette reflected the minister's short period in office. It, too, was like a passing shadow, a silhouette!

666, THE NUMBER OF THE BEAST

Periods of political upheaval and cataclysm often have been regarded as the work of satanic powers. It was thought that no human could cause such disastrous conditions, leading the world to the very brink of destruction. For almost 2000 years, the evil-bringing force has been identified with the apocalyptic 'Beast'. To add to the mystery, it has been said that its number is '666'.

Its origin is a passage in the Book of Revelation (13:18) which gives some indication as to the meaning of the puzzling numerical reference:

He that hath understanding, let him count the number of the beast: for it is the number of a man; and his number is Six Hundred and Sixty Six.

The number specifically refers to a person—not a supernatural demonic force such as Satan or Antichrist, as is sometimes assumed.

The Book of Revelation, the last book in the New Testament, is in majority a series of visions. They deal with the terror and disaster at the end of time when, in a last battle with the forces of evil, the divine power will triumph, to establish a New Heaven and a New Earth.

A period of great worry, people still vividly remembered the terror of the fall of Jerusalem and the suffering that Nero's persecution had caused. St John, no doubt, wrote the

Apocalypse (by which name the Book of Revelation is also known) to give courage and comfort to the young Christian community. When human power was at its wits' end, divine intervention would save the world by establishing a new era, cleansed from evil and ruled by the divine spirit.

To understand the relevant passage, it is necessary to realise that John was well acquainted with Jewish tradition and, no doubt, with a particular characteristic of the Hebrew language. Like Greek, the letters of the Hebrew alphabet double up as figures, the A standing for '1', the B for '2', and so on. Therefore, every name (or word) has a numerical value as well, easily ascertained by adding up the letter-figures of which the name consists.

Applying this method to a common name of today, the number for Smith (with the name spelled out in Hebrew), would be 124, the total achieved by adding up the value of the S (60), the M (40), the I (10), the T (9) and the H (5).

S	M	I	T	H
60	40	10	9	5 = 124

Experience throughout history further clarifies the employment of this method of coding in political circumstances. Ruthless dictators outlawed any criticism. Whoever dared to criticise would be punished by imprisonment, exile or execution. However, freedom-loving people then, as now, would not be silenced. Unable to voice their opinions openly, they learnt to use secret symbols, or cryptograms. The peculiar faculty of the Hebrew alphabet easily lent itself to such a code. People just replaced the name too dangerous to be mentioned with its numerical value! Contemporaries had no difficulty in identifying who the 'figure' represented.

Present-day readers can only guess which tyrant was meant by '666'. The Book of Revelation was written during a tumultuous period when many tyrants were trying to gain the upper hand. Identifying who was meant by '666' is a hazardous task which may easily lead to error or misinterpretation. It is no wonder that the number of the beast has been said to refer to, or to prophesy, many people throughout history. These include Emperor Hadrian, the Pope, Napoleon, Martin Luther and even some twentieth-century heads of state!

However, the most plausible suggestion points to Nero Caesar. Spelt out in Hebrew characters (in which initially only consonants were used), the letters of his name add up to 666:

N	R	W	N	K	S	R
50	200	6	50	100	60	200 = 666

There is another, and much less complex, explanation. Traditionally, '7' was regarded a sacred figure. It was 'the perfect number'. But when reduced by one it changed into its opposite. With one digit less for each number—666—it was thought to represent 'the man of sin'—the Antichrist.

SKELETON IN THE CUPBOARD

To exhume a body used to be against the law and carried heavy penalties. That it was regarded as a serious offence was based on ancient tradition and superstition. It was thought that to unearth a corpse was a most dangerous undertaking, threatening the entire community. It might cause the soul of the dead to be disturbed and, once released, haunt the living. Religiously too it was abhorrent, decried as a desecration of the dead and one's last resting place. The only bodies exempt were those of executed criminals.

The prohibition severely limited medical training and research. For the sake of their anatomical studies, doctors therefore engaged professional grave robbers who, for a high price and, of course, illegally, dug up bodies. Bizarrely they became known as resurrection-men.

To avoid discovery of their grisly possession, the doctors hid the skeletons in the closets of their homes. And it was this 'skeleton in the cupboard' which came to serve not only anatomy but daily speech. Many people were thought to have a private secret, something they did not want others to know. There was no better metaphor to depict their concealment than that of the doctors' 'skeleton in the cupboard'.

Though the Anatomy Act of 1832 permitted the exhumation of bodies, and there was no longer any need for their bones to be hidden away in closets, the 'skeleton in the cupboard' survived in the phraseology of everyday speech.

SKULL AND CROSSBONES

Among the most fear-inspiring symbols is that of a skull and crossed bones. Emblem of mortality and death, it is still used as a warning of fatal danger. No words are necessary to explain its meaning. Even illiterates understand its message.

They were once displayed on the flags of ships, to indicate the outbreak of a life-threatening disease on board. Pirates used it as their symbol on their flag. It became part of some military uniforms. It was also adopted as the distinguishing badge of the Nazi storm troopers, the dreaded SS.

The emblem of skull and crossbones also played a part in the symbolism of religious faith and ancient mystery cults. They served them as a reminder of the transience of life on earth, prompting the faithful to contemplate their mortality, to practise penitence and renounce this world.

Positively, it expressed a powerful message of solace and of hope. The preservation of the skull and two legbones of a deceased was believed to ensure their resurrection.

SLAPSTICK

Slapstick humour obtained its name from a simple stratagem of nineteenth-century comedians and clowns to amuse their audience and raise laughs. They used two sticks tied together at one end, but loose at the other. With this they struck the rear end of their victim, not once, but many times. Skilfully 'performed', each time the impact on the posterior of the dupe (in reality a partner) thus castigated produced a resounding noise.

The sticks, though no longer used, survive in what is now called 'slapstick' comedy, with its horseplay and maltreatment of the various characters.

SLIPSHOD

Anything 'slipshod' is carelessly made. The word goes back to the (mispronounced) slipshoes, at one time the name of loosely-fitting slippers. Not laced up, they were very much like modern loafers. Worn only at home, it was unfitting to be seen in them in the street.

In the sixteenth century, however, people got lackadaisical and did not care very much about their appearance. All they were concerned about was their comfort. So they did not mind keeping their slipshoes on, even when they slipped outside. But those among the population who still appreciated the niceties of life considered such people disrespectful and uncouth, and their untidy dress as despicable. To be slipshoed became a description of the slattern, eventually further to deteriorate linguistically from slipshoed to slipshod, applied to anything done in a haphazard, slovenly manner.

Slogan

Slogans act as messages. Catch phrases, they advertise goods or popular causes. Concise and to the point, rhythmic and startling, they are easily remembered.

To start with, however, a slogan was not used for the promotion of merchandise or to express and spread an ideological view or policy. The slogan was the Scots' battlecry for which, at times, they used the name of their clan or leader. Advancing against the enemy, the men joined in stridently and in unison, repeating it numerous times. They did so with a triple purpose: to galvanise themselves into action, to confront the enemy in a state of almost frenzy, and by their cries to scare the adversary into submission. Not surprisingly, the original Gaelic words out of which grew the now so peaceful slogan, *sluagh ghairm*, meant an 'army shout' or a 'war cry'.

Slush fund

Slush funds are a phenomenon of modern, corrupt society. Their money—unaccounted for—is used to buy votes or the goodwill of people who, lacking integrity, are prepared for a price to do or say whatever is asked of them. It is dirty money, indeed, murky like slush and the name chosen for it most appropriate. However, surprisingly, for slush to sink so low is only a comparatively recent development.

The original slush funds, established in the nineteenth century, were not hidden accounts nor had they any political connotation or association with bribes. They started at sea and were above board. Slush to sailors was the refuse from their ship's galley, primarily the waste grease or fat of the meat left over after it had been cooked. It became their rightful property which they were permitted to sell. The money collected from the proceeds they called their slush fund which they used to buy themselves extra luxuries.

The word slush comes from a Scandinavian root for 'mud' or 'filth' or any 'sloppy matter'.

SNOB

A snob is an arrogant, pompous upstart who actually says so themselves—but in Latin.

Even the name is not real, but a combination of two abbreviations. In days gone by, in class-ridden Britain, some of the Cambridge colleges requested that those registering as students had to add their rank to their name. Commoners, not of noble blood, were obliged to record the fact by noting down on the college list that they were 'without nobility'. They had to do so in Latin, *sine nobilitate*. With insufficient space, they shortened their (dis)qualification by putting instead S.*nob*.

It did not take long to drop the full stop and, by combining the two abbreviations, give birth to the *snob*. When the latter started to imitate his noble classmates, pretending to be like them, a member of the aristocracy, it gave the snob its present-day meaning.

Thackeray is believed to have been the first to use 'snob'. He did so, not very deferentially nor loyally, in conferring the title on King George IV!

SOLSTICE

Twice every year, the sun—in its imagined circuit around the earth—seems to come to a halt. This occurs when it reaches the southernmost and the northernmost distance from the equator. According to the hemisphere, the occasion is known as the summer or the winter solstice. The term solstice, literally describing the event, is derived from a combination of the Latin *sol* for 'sun' and *stitium* for 'standing still'. It thus speaks of the solar 'standstill'.

Calendar-wise, the phenomenon coincides with 21 June and 21 December respectively, being regarded as the beginning of summer or winter, depending on the hemisphere, northern or southern. The dates are postponed by one day whenever a leap year follows.

The apparent standstill of the sun did not go unnoticed. In fact, for thousands of years, people anxiously used to watch the occurrence. They were deeply concerned that the solar body would not get stuck but return, as they were well aware how much their very existence depended on its warmth and light. They did whatever they could, particularly so at the time of the winter solstice, to help the sun to turn around. The magic they employed is still re-enacted (though rationalised) in some of the Christmas customs, such as the burning of the yule log and the firing of the pudding.

Rituals linked with the summer solstice equally have left their mark and are continued to be observed to this very day in some parts of the world. Best-known of all the ceremonies held at that time are those at the ancient sun sanctuary of Stonehenge, England, situated near the cathedral city of Salisbury.

SOW WILD OATS

Youths (mostly males) are said to 'sow wild oats' when, prior to settling down they lead a lifestyle of permissiveness and indulgence, doing so adventurously and often irresponsibly. Though it must be remembered that 'wild' has meant many things throughout the years. In days past, one didn't have to do much to be so regarded.

The phrase itself is a peculiar choice of words. Anything

growing wild is not cultivated. How then could anyone sow wild oats? But the very paradox was meant to stress the youths' folly in spending precious time and energy on things that had no lasting value. Wild oats were worth very little. They were just weeds.

Even the horse might have had a share in the creation of the saying. Feeding on lots of oats made it specially frisky and, it was believed, in its state of wildness, sexually highly roused. In like manner, youths sowing their wild oats became impetuous and intensely ardent and, anxious to prove their adulthood by sexual prowess, did not hold back.

Now regarded as a mere phase of life and accepted as 'natural', once upon a time 'sowing one's wild oats' was not only condemned morally but decried as a mistake. The only result of the pursuit was a worthless crop of weeds—'wild oats'!

SPEAKEASY

The name of the 'speakeasy', the unlicensed club which, illegally, serves liquor, goes back to the days of American prohibition. Establishments circumventing the law and selling drinks were so called. Hidden away and well-guarded by the profiteers running them, they were well known to the 'informed'.

To gain entry, would-be customers had to have good recommendations. They were admitted only by a password, whispered to the doorkeeper. Colloquially, to speak softly and with a quiet voice was to 'speak easy'.

There is also an opinion which claims that though the term was popularised in the United States, it originated in the English underworld. Smugglers' haunts there were known, at least as early as 1823, as 'speak-softly shops'. Among the goods they supplied—on the quiet—was cheap liquor.

Spick and span

Anything smart, trim and spruce, is 'spick and span' or, as it was initially called, 'spick and span new'.

A 'span' was a chip of wood, freshly cut from a tree. Often serving as a spoon, never having been used before or for any other purpose, it was thoroughly clean and completely new,

A 'spick' was a spike or nail. Just as the wooden chip was entirely new, so the spike came straight from the blacksmith's anvil. (Germans still speak of something as *Nagelneu*.) It has even been suggested that, next to the wooden spoon (span), the spike might have once served as a complementary eating implement, a primitive kind of fork.

Another derivation links anything span-new (developed from the Anglo-Saxon *spanna*) with the weaving of cloth. It had been 'spun new' and came straight from the loom!

Going back to the sea, 'spick and span' has also been claimed as relating to the beauty of a new ship which, with all its timber and its nails totally new, looked sparkling and stately.

'Spick' and 'span' thus said the same thing—only in different ways. Reinforcing each other, no doubt they were specially joined because of their attractive alliteration.

Spill the beans

Beans grew plentifully in American soil and served the country's indigenous people and early European settlers as wholesome food. This explains why in everyday speech beans were used as a general metaphor. In the 1830s, for instance, Americans spoke of those who were ill-informed or totally ignorant of a matter that they 'did not know beans'. On the other hand, people admired for their shrewdness and wisdom were described as 'knowing how many beans make five'.

This usage, most likely, was responsible for the now common description of revealing a secret prematurely as 'spilling the beans'. It too comes from the United States, where it was first employed in the early 1900s.

Popular, but apocryphal, is the claim that the phrase is based on a practice of secret societies in antiquity. Esoteric communities in ancient Greece admitted a new member only if agreed upon by a majority vote of the initiates. They indicated their acceptance or rejection of the candidate in a secret ballot. Each voter was given two beans: a white one, to be counted as affirmative, and a brown (or black) one, as dissent. The beans were cast into a ballot box, initially a simple jar of a helmet, then counted in secret. The candidate receiving a majority of white beans was accepted. However, no one was ever to know the actual number of white or dark beans cast which left the newly-chosen member ignorant of how many had voted for or against him.

Occasionally, by an untoward accident the receptacle was knocked over and, by 'spilling the beans', disclosed what had been meant to be a secret.

SPINSTER

Spinster was the official designation of a female who had never been married before. The term, now mostly discarded, originally reflected a significant practice. It goes back to the time when a girl had to provide and actually to make her own trousseau.

In pre-industrial days, the manufacture of textiles was mainly a cottage industry. Not surprisingly therefore, with women not going out to work, the girl was expected to spin the yarn from the fleece of sheep which she then weaved into cloth for her outfit and bed linen. In fact, she was regarded suitable to serve (!) as a wife only when she had spun all the cloth needed to cover her body, the table and the bed. It was for this reason that unmarried girls became known as the 'spinners' or 'spinsters'. No wonder that Alfred the Great called the women of his house the 'spindle side'.

The trousseau, obviously a French word, actually refers to the 'little bundle' of clothes the girl prepared, whilst still a 'spinster'.

SPITTING IMAGE

A confusion of language and the slurring of speech have largely been held responsible for the creation of the 'spitting image', a rather odd choice as a figure of speech.

When, in the Deep South of America, blacks wanted to give comfort to a child bereaved of its father, they complimented it by remarking how much it looked like him. This they expressed by saying that it was 'the very spirit and image of its dad'. In their drawl, the word sounded like 'the very spit an' image'. It did not take long for people to take them literally.

Originally, according to another derivation, the spitting image was a 'splitting' image. Just as splinters from a tree look very much alike, so did those so depicted.

There is also a suggestion that the phrase is a corruption of 'spit and image'. Improper enunciation then changed the 'spit and image' into 'spit'n image', eventually resulting in the mystifying 'spitting image'. Intended to stress the striking resemblance of two people, very realistically it stated that they were as much alike as two drops of saliva.

In early times (and still in some remote regions), saliva was considered a sacred substance. It was part of a person's soul and spirit. No wonder that it was used to heal, to make the blind see or—in primitive magic—to dominate a person by getting possession of some of his spittle. People who wanted to stress the striking likeness of a child were thus well justified to remark that it was like the very spittle out of its father's mouth, part of his very substance and soul.

SQUARE

The geometric figure of the square came to play a significant function as a figure of speech as well, experiencing a change of meaning as the years went by.

Initially American slang, an honest person was called a 'square'. Appropriately, among card players, a 'square deal' acknowledged that whoever had dealt the cards had not cheated. Those praised for their square talk spoke the truth—outright and plain.

The carpenter's tool, no doubt, suggested its specific linguistic use. His square enabled him to draw straight lines. They did not deviate, were not crooked or even slightly bent.

Theodore Roosevelt picked up the word, to give it wide currency and make it popular. The first time he used it was in 1901. Urging federal curbs on the new United Steel Corporation, he demanded that 'big business give people a square deal'. Three years later, he once again employed it during his presidential campaign of 1904. In a speech he made in Washington, he promised that, if elected, he would see to it 'that every man had a square deal, no more, no less'.

In the early 1940s, jazz musicians adopted the term. However, they gave it a totally different connotation. 'Squares' to them were the people who, set in their ways and with closed minds, failed to appreciate the type of music they had introduced. The novel interpretation of the word was eventually taken up by the new generation of hippies and beatniks. Condescendingly they attached the label to those too old-fashioned to understand and appreciate their lifestyle, likening them to 'square pegs in round holes'.

Theirs was not a new metaphor. It had first been asserted by Sydney Smith, the nineteenth century clergyman and essayist, renowned for his wit displayed both in his conversation and writings. He had discussed in his *Sketches of Moral Philosophy* (published in 1806) the various types of people and the necessity to find for them their proper place in life. In doing so, he made use of a simple metaphor. He compared the opportunities life offered with holes made in a table top. Of different shapes, they were circular, triangular, oblong and square. Individuals, on the other hand, were like bits of wood, equally diverse. Unfortunately, it sometimes happened that they were placed in the wrong type of hole which did not match. A square person thus might (try to) squeeze themselves into a round hole.

The comparison soon caught on and 'square' was adopted as the description or designation of a misfit.

For a new generation which regarded itself as up-to-date and well-rounded, it was not far-fetched or difficult to decry those not recognising their advanced lifestyle as being (such) squares. They did not fit into the new world. Apart from it, there was nothing rounded in their way of life. Everything they did was cornered, jagged and time-worn.

Other explanations exist as to how the square acquired its modern connotation. At one time, a dull-witted person was nicknamed a 'squarehead'. People actually believed that an inferior mind was reflected in an abnormal, unrounded shape of the person's head. Ultimately, the 'head' was dropped, which left the square as a term of reproach for those 'out of step' with the latest.

Going to the other extreme, square was also used for an intellectual. This was done, it was explained, because it reminded people of the square-shaped mortarboard of academic dress.

To dub people disapprovingly as 'squares' in the sense of their being out-of-date and totally antiquated has also been seen as the result of their no longer being 'with it'. They still enjoyed square dancing, long after it had gone out of fashion.

STADIUM

Stadion, a Greek word, once was a standard measure of length. It was a distance of 184 metres (613 ft), covered in footraces run at Delphi, Olympia and Athens and other notable sporting sites.

Subsequently, the racing track itself was called after it. This was the beginning of the modern stadium. Its location was chosen mainly in a natural depression, so that it was flanked by upward sloping ground or embankments on either end of the course. This enabled the spectators to watch the runners' progress from an elevated position. To start with, the visitors just squatted down on the ground. Eventually, they were provided with seats. In a further development, the whole area was enclosed by a wall, for the entire complex to be called by the measure—*stadion*.

The Romans took over both the idea and the term, Latinising the latter into stadium, a name that has been adopted and retained universally. Its function, however, has expanded greatly. No longer reserved for footraces alone, the stadium became the arena for a great number of sporting events.

The once naturally shaped and utilitarian meeting place was then converted into amphitheatres, some so exquisite that they were described as architectural extravaganzas. One stadium in Rome accommodated 50 000 spectators. Its seats were of marble. It was elaborately decorated and displayed spectacular statuary. At Athens, at enormous cost, Herodes Atticus built (in AD 177) a stadium of equal splendour as his gift to the city.

STAG PARTY

The modern stag party, known in Australia as a bucks' party, arranged as a send-off to a friend about to be married, is the last link in a long chain of male domination. It goes back to the custom of excluding women from tribal gatherings. The main reason for the discrimination was fear. This was based on a physiological phenomenon that, not understood, mystified and frightened man. The blood that periodically issued from a woman's body was regarded a threatening substance and a source of defilement. Her very presence therefore was imagined to spell misfortune. Ignorance of the facts of menstruation was the beginning of separation and exclusion of women. It has been perpetuated through the millennia in all types of gatherings, societies and clubs.

Men invented their own excuses for their male chauvinism. They said it was to save the women embarrassment at obscene jokes and talk that was off-colour, particularly in the case of a stag party prior to the nuptials.

STARK NAKED

That anyone wearing no clothes whatsoever is described as 'stark naked' is due to an old Anglo-Saxon word that originally (and still in the thirteenth century) did not sound like 'stark' at all. It was *steort*, pronounced more like 'start' and referred to the 'rump and tail'. Whoever was 'stark naked', therefore, was completely in the nude—even to the (metaphorical) tail.

Stepmother and Stepfather

Misunderstood and misrepresented is the name and role of step-parents. The prefix in their title does not refer to any 'step', leading upward or downward, in the scale of their relationship or the 'degree' they occupy in the family tree.

More human, it recalls the reason for their assuming this—at times—thankless function. From Old English, the 'step', in their case, means 'bereavement'. It records the fact that one's real mother or father has passed away and that the 'bereaved' parent has remarried. Hence the new mother or father, no longer blood-related, has come to occupy her or his position through the bereavement. The sad circumstance was recalled in the name, when its meaning was still recognised.

It is sad enough to lose one's parent, but an additional source of deep regret is the bad reputation given, often undeservedly, to the person taking her or his place. The association of step-parents with being cruel and unkind is not the result of real experience. Fairytales, such as Cinderella, have been responsible for it. Read out in the nursery, these stories, mostly depicting a stepmother as a horrible creature, have left their mark in the mind of the adult. It shows what fiction can do, and how feelings and attitudes acquired in early childhood condition people's outlook and the emotive effect of words and names for the rest of their lives.

Stiff upper lip

For a person, particularly a man, to show emotion, especially among the British, used to be regarded as unfitting and undignified. It proved a lack of maturity and self-discipline. But to do so as a member of the armed forces would be all the more degrading.

In spite of it, not everyone succeeded and, without being aware of it, gave away their inner feelings. On the brink of bursting out in tears, but withholding them, their lips would tremble. This movement became all the more noticeable at a time when fashion made young soldiers sport moustaches, so common then that they almost seemed to be part of their uniform. To make them even more conspicuous, they were kept stiff by the application of wax. This practice had one disadvantage. The very rigidity of the moustache drew attention to the least movement of the upper lip, of which the slightest twitch revealed that the man was under stress.

To keep a stiff upper lip therefore became a military necessity. Eventually adopted as a metaphor in civilian life, it portrayed the ability to keep oneself under control in the most adverse of circumstances.

STONY BROKE

Someone who is completely down and out, unable to pay their bills, is colloquially called 'stony broke' or, in the United States, 'stone broke'. The strange description is said by some to have started among craftsmen. When unable to meet their obligations, they had their stone bench broken. Quite literally, thus, they were stone broke.

The explanation would confine such fate—at least originally—to one specific class of workmen. Unfortunately, insolvency can strike anyone. Therefore an alternative interpretation of the term seems more acceptable. It recalls the use of 'stony' in general speech as an intensive, adding emphasis. People completely bereft of hearing are called 'stone deaf' and those who cannot see at all are 'stone blind'. Since there are degrees of wealth, so poverty, too, has its degrees. Some people are plain broke, others, entirely impecunious, are stony-broke.

Straw that broke the camel's back

The camel is renowned as a beast of burden and has served people through the millennia most often in arid countries. It is known for its ability to go without water for long periods of time. But even with all its power of endurance, it reaches a limit when 'enough is enough'.

Mostly a camel can carry up to a maximum of 450 kg (1000 lb) in weight. But a single straw then added to it would break its back. It is the 'final straw'.

The animal's example served as a poignant warning to everyone not to go beyond the point of no return. Once having reach the extent of their stamina, even the hardiest of people break down. The smallest of incidents will change a calamity into a catastrophe. It would be like the straw that broke the camel's back.

It has been suggested that the saying is an adaptation of Charles Dickens' reference to 'the last straw [that] breaks the laden camel's back' in *Dombey and Son*, which he wrote in 1847–8. On his part, Dickens could have been influenced in its choice by a passage in the works of the seventeenth-century English clergyman Thomas Fuller. A clever and prolific author, the reverend was noted for his gift in compressing shrewd observations into memorable, quaintly humoured aphorisms. In one of these he had expressed the thought that "Tis the last feather that breaks the horse's back'. Not mixing the breeds, as it were, it must have seemed to Dickens so much more feasible to change the feather into 'the last straw', and the horse into the camel.

Actually, the phrase can be traced to a discussion said to have taken place in the seventeenth century. It concerned the limit of tolerance eventually reached by everyone. As an illustration it quoted an experiment done with a camel, measuring the maximum amount of weight it could carry. To ascertain it, the animal's load was increased very gradually and slowly, by adding one straw each time. It was so light and little, that it really did not seem to matter. Ultimately, however, the stage was reached when just one more straw—the 'last' one—broke the animal's back.

STRIKE WHILE THE IRON IS HOT

Idioms and sayings are time-conditioned. Observations of everyday occurrences often serve to illustrate and underscore an idea. But changing times and circumstances as well as the advance of civilisation make many practices obsolete and any reference to them meaningless to a new generation. Nevertheless, language is slow in adjusting and updating itself and continues to employ metaphors that, once clear and obvious, have become puzzling and obscure.

A typical example is the advice not to postpone an action when the most opportune moment for it has come, by counselling to 'strike while the iron is hot'. To present-day society the iron would suggest the appliance used for pressing fabrics and clothes, in which context the saying makes little sense. However, at the time it was coined, everybody understood it. Blacksmiths then fulfilled an essential function in the community. When shoeing horses, they could hammer (strike) the iron into the required shape only while it was still red hot.

STUMBLING BLOCK

To call an obstacle standing in one's way a stumbling block is the result of missionary zeal and, hence, part of the history of religion.

To make a message stick in people's mind, the message given will make use of a striking phrase and some popular metaphor, easily comprehended and remembered by those addressed.

St Paul did so in one of his letters which are now part of the New Testament. Written to the young Christian community in Rome, he tried to impress on its members how much they needed each other. In his Epistle to the Romans (14:13) he exhorted them to be mindful not to put any obstruction into each other's way. To underscore his admonition and make it all the more memorable, he employed a term used in hunting, then a popular pursuit among the Romans. He asked the new Christians in the city not to put 'a spring of a trap' (*skandalon*) in their brothers' path. Everyone would know what he meant.

When Tyndale (1492–1536) translated the Greek text of the New Testament into English, he realised that *skandalon* had become a meaningless word to his generation. At his time, people no longer trapped animals by means of springs. For this reason, he changed the obsolete term to a word which would be understood immediately. Substituting the original phrase, he altered the traditional text, but did not change its sense. In his 'translation' the passage read that they should not put 'a stumbling block' in their brothers' path.

So simple a word, it was the most appropriate description, soon to be adopted generally in English. The subsequent King James edition of the Bible adopted Tyndale's novel idiom and did so in eleven different cases. Thus, the 'stumbling block' became part and parcel of English speech without people being aware that it had all started by a Bible translator's desire to make scripture a living document for his time and, with this purpose in mind, had rendered its text not only accurately but colloquially. A perfect translation is not translating words alone, but the meaning of them.

STUMPED

The stump is a small leftover of a felled tree, still stuck in the ground. Hence, to stump a person by asking them questions they are unable to answer reduces them, as it were, to a stump of their former impressive stature which could be compared with tall trees. So to speak, they are being cut down to size.

Alternately, the choice of words may recall an early experience of settlers on wooded land. Felling huge trees to prepare the ground for cultivation, stumps left were so deeply embedded and of such girth that the men, lacking modern machinery, were at their wits' end how to remove them. They were truly 'stumped'!

SUCKER

The sucker is a person so naive and gullible that they are easily deceived. How the nickname was given has prompted a variety of explanations.

A person's innocence and simplicity of mind has been compared to that of a baby, still *sucking* its mother's milk.

Fish have equally been given the credit for being responsible for the word. During early white settlement in the United States, the pioneers' attention was soon drawn to a peculiar type of fish. By protracting its toothless mouth with its fleshy lips it seemed to suck up its food from the beds of the lakes. This made them call the fish a sucker. Plentiful (at least 60 of its species have been identified in North America), the fish were easily caught. True sportsmen regarded them as too easy a prey. The least experienced angler could catch a 'sucker'!

It did not take long for its name to be transferred to humans who also bite when a conman throws them a bait. Well-known is the observation, commonly attributed to Phineas Barnum (d. 1891), the famous American showman, that 'there is a sucker born every minute'. Whether he really said so is uncertain, but it is known that he was convinced that people like to be taken in, to be 'humbugged'.

SWEEPSTAKE

In a sweepstake the lucky individual who has backed the winner 'sweeps up' the whole amount (or a substantial part) staked by all the other betters. The choice of word almost conveys the exhilaration of the fortunate person who collects the money 'in one sweep'.

Best-known of all are the Irish Sweeps. Ironically (or typically Irish), they were held on the occasion of English horseraces, particularly the Derby and Grand National Steeple Chase, and the tickets sold for them were mostly purchased outside Ireland! However, a quarter of the takings was used for the upkeep of Irish hospitals.

Though, initially, the winner of a game or race swept the total amount of stakes into their pocket, the 'sweep' then became a shared venture, with prizes divided according to value.

Several puzzling features still unresolved are part of the sweepstake. Though sweepstakes in the modern sense date back only to the eighteenth century, Sweepstake as a family name is listed in a 1379 poll-tax register. Naval records show that a ship was so called in 1495. One is left to wonder as to the origin and meaning of the name at that time.

SYCOPHANT

A sycophant who, by servile flattery, tries to gain some advantage from an influential person, literally is 'showing a fig'. The reason for this Greek-derived description may be manifold.

The sign of a fig, clandestinely made by the fingers of one's hand, pointed to a person whom (rightly or falsely) one accused of a misdemeanour. More specifically, a sycophant was an informer against people who, at a time when the export of figs from Athens was prohibited, ignoring the law, sold them abroad. By handing over the smuggler to the authorities, the sycophant expected special favours from them.

Another theory suggests that the name can be traced to the time when fig trees were regarded as sacred and no ordinary person was permitted to pick their fruit. A sycophant gave away those who blasphemously and selfishly had done so nevertheless. No doubt in return they hoped to receive a reward—either from the gods or those representing them.

'Sycophant' thus goes back a long way and in the process completely changed its meaning. Once an informer and accuser, the name has come down to assume the position of a bootlicker, a back-scratcher and a toady.

TABBY CAT

TAKEN FOR A RIDE

TARMAC

TARRED WITH THE SAME BRUSH

TAXI

TEA BAGS

TEDDY BEAR

THAT TAKES THE CAKE

THIRD DEGREE

THREE MISFORTUNES IN A ROW

TICKER TAPE

TICKLED PINK

TIERED WEDDING CAKE

TILL THE COWS COME HOME

TIPPLER

TIPSY

TOFF

TOILET

TOILET PAPER

TOM CAT

TONGUE IN CHEEK

TOSSING A COIN

TRIVIA

TRUTH IS STRANGER THAN FICTION

TURN THE TABLES

TURNCOAT

TWO STRINGS TO A BOW

TABBY CAT

Some cats, like the Siamese and Burmese, highly prized (and priced), proudly proclaim by their name the country popularly assumed to be their homeland. A tabby cat is different. Its ancestry apparently is unattached to any specific part of the world. Nonetheless, its name goes back to Mesopotamia, Abraham's home, the site of the most ancient culture, the modern Iraq. Its link with that historic land, however, is not one of a blood relationship. It is an involved chain of events, showing the rich heritage of even a simple striped cat.

Attabiya was a district of Baghdad, named after Attab, a medieval Arab prince. The suburb developed into an industrial centre. A silken dress fabric manufactured there and distinguished by its striped pattern, appropriately was called after the suburb, *attabi*, and exported as such. The French sold it as *tabis* which on the English market became tabby cloth. The pattern of the material resembled the markings of a striped cat so much that this feline soon was named after it—to become the tabby!

TAKEN FOR A RIDE

Nowadays if someone is being 'taken for a ride', they are being cheated, deceived or tricked. Mostly, the victim chosen is a simpleton or a gullible sort of person. Originally, the expression was meant literally. People were taken for a ride in a car. However, theirs was a one-way trip.

During American gang warfare, members who had fallen out with the 'boss' were sent for to meet the leader, they were told, to settle matters. They got into the car—but never returned.

TARMAC

A peculiar sort of amalgam is the name of the tarmac, the runway used by aircraft for their take-off and landing. It joins 'tar' to the first syllable of *mac*adamised. The choice of word pays tribute to an early pioneer in road building, while simultaneously taking note of an essential improvement, the addition of tar.

John Loudon McAdam (also spelled Macadam), a Scotsman by birth (in 1756), already as a child had been interested in the smooth flowing of traffic. In the backyard of his home, he built a model road. When John was only 14, his father died and he joined his uncle in the United States. Eventually he returned to Britain to settle down in Ayrshire, where he was made a magistrate and a road trustee. Almost immediately he resumed his childhood pursuit—now seriously. Aware of the neglect of the mostly dirt roads and appalled by their condition which caused great damage to coaches, he set out to find some way to make the traffic lanes of Britain roadworthy. In 1827, he was appointed general surveyor of roads of the English highways.

He travelled 48 000 kilometres (30 000 miles) and spent £5000 out of his own pocket on experiments. The end result was his invention of a novel process that ensured a more stable and resistant surface for roads. After putting down several layers of crushed stones, these were compressed by means of heavy rollers, providing a much superior kind of highway. The weight of the coaches passing over it did no damage: on the contrary they further consolidated it. His method was soon recognised as an extraordinary advance in road construction, to be referred to as 'macadamisation'.

A final improvement came about in 1901 by mere accident. While on an inspection tour, E.P. Hooley, a Midlands county surveyor, was struck by the fact that a short section of one road was far better preserved than the rest. Puzzled, he pursued the matter, to be told that not long ago at that very spot a barrel of tar had fallen off a dray, with all its contents being spilled. Unable easily to remove the spillage, workers had done the next best thing and covered up the tar with slag they had obtained from nearby iron works. No one had noticed the result, prior to the surveyor. Having ascertained the circumstances, he lost little time in making use of them. Within two years, he formed a company to construct the new type of road. He called his firm the Tar Macadam Syndicate. Shortened, it created the modern 'tarmac'.

TARRED WITH THE SAME BRUSH

People sharing common faults or traits are said to be 'tarred with the same brush'. The words, carrying now a disparaging meaning, may have been suggested by one of several practices.

At one time, felons or political opponents, to be easily recognised and publicly penalised with their body stripped naked, were 'tarred and feathered'. Naturally, the same brush was applied to all of them.

Cattle could easily be identified by their owner by branding them with their mark. This, however, could not be done to sheep. It would damage their fleece. Instead, these were tarred distinctly at a specific spot, done of course with the same brush.

Animals who suffered from sores or ticks were equally treated. To heal their open wounds or protect them from the vermin, they too were tarred with the same brush.

TAXI

The taxi started on its very first trip as a taxi-meter cab. It happened in New York City on 25 October 1907 and was the result of a New Yorker's anger at being grossly overcharged for a short ride in one of the horse-drawn hansom cabs that were then plying their trade.

Harry Allen, on his way home, felt so exhausted that, though he had not far to go, he decided to use a cab. Arriving at his destination, he could not believe his ears when he was asked to pay $5 for the fare, an exorbitant charge in those days for so short a ride.

On the spot he determined once and for all to stop such exploitation. He would introduce a new service for commuters from one part of the city to another, in which passengers paid a fare fixed according to the distance covered and based on a 'tariff' or 'tax' (from the French *taxe* for 'charge') measured in units. The distance covered was not left to guesswork, but was accurately calculated by a meter. At the end of the journey, this indicated the mileage driven. There would be no chance left for overcharging.

Appropriately, Harry Allen called his new type of conveyance a taxi-meter cab. Universally adopted, it went different ways in the various parts of the world. Too cumbersome in its name, a portion of it was dropped. Some retained the 'cab' and others, the 'taxi'.

Allen admitted that he had adopted the idea of the taxi (and the word) from a French company which produced meters for horse-drawn cabs and had first coined the term *taximetre* for its intricate device (invented in France c. 1898) to 'clock' the exact charge. All he had done was to join the 'taxi' to his cab.

TEA BAGS

Tea bags are American-born. They came into existence through both the economic prudency of a tea merchant and a misunderstanding on the part of the public.

In 1904, an enterprising businessman selling tea had the idea to advertise his merchandise by sending free samples to potential customers. To present each with a tin container then generally used would have proved much too costly. He therefore decided to have instead some loose tea sewn into small silk bags.

His would-be clients misinterpreted the promotion. Lacking any printed explanation, they did not realise that the bags were mini-pockets from which the tea was meant to be emptied out into a pot. They thought that they were expected to brew it by pouring boiling water on to those—not to be opened—advertising bags.

Doing so, they found that it was a much faster method to prepare a cup of tea. It also enabled them to dispose of the used tea leaves so much more easily.

When orders for the novel tea bags 'poured' in, the astute tea merchant began to manufacture the filter paper tea bags which, nowadays, are taken for granted, but had never really been intended to become a permanent feature.

TEDDY BEAR

Presidents of the United States may be remembered for many things. But none, possibly, equals in fame Theodore 'Teddy' Roosevelt. It was not short-lived, merely lasting for the tenure of his office, but has continued to this day—in every nursery. His gift to all people, whether young in years or in heart, was the teddy bear.

In 1902, the second year of his presidency, he paid an

official visit to Mississippi. His intention was to settle a border-dispute between that state and adjacent Louisiana. In between strenuous negotiations, he took some time off to relax, and went hunting.

On the outing, he unexpectedly came across a small bear cub that had taken refuge in a tree not far off. He could easily have shot it. But he regarded this as cruel and unsportsman-like. Without hesitation, he lowered his gun and let the cub go free.

It did not take long for the media to get hold of the story. Clifford K. Berryman, cartoonist for the *Washington Evening Star*, immortalised the incident in an appealing sketch. It showed the president in a posture in which while downing his gun, he was raising his hand toward the little furry creature. The artist captioned the picture with the telling words—so appropriate in the circumstances of his mission—'Where the president draws the line.' No doubt, ingeniously, the political inference of the words was Roosevelt's intervention in the borderline dispute between the two states.

Americans are astute business people and before long Morris Mitchom, a Russian immigrant who had a toyshop in Brooklyn, commercialised the incident. From brown plush he made a small bear. To attract customers, he placed it in his show window. He then wrote to the president asking for permission to call the little animal after him. In his reply, 'Teddy' Roosevelt gladly conceded, though expressing the view that he did not think that his name 'is worth much in the toy bear-cub business'. Thus the 'teddy' bear came into existence to give joy and pleasure to countless children everywhere.

Another slightly different version tells that Roosevelt had gone to Mississippi specifically to hunt bears. To please the president, his hosts made sure of his quarry. On the very first day of his visit, they captured a small brown bear which, surreptitiously, they released just prior to the president's arrival, thereby presenting him with an easy target. Catching sight of the lovely creature, however, he took pity on it and, without knowing of the ruse, did not fire, but made sure that the little creature got away.

THAT TAKES THE CAKE

Something outstanding and extraordinarily remarkable—in fact, something so fantastic that it is almost beyond belief—is said to 'take the cake'. Though the expression goes back to a practice in classical times of awarding a cake to a successful contestant, it assumed its modern connotation in the deep south of the United States in the days of slavery.

Among the favourite pastimes of the blacks was a competition which took the form of a 'walk-around' or 'parade'. It was known as the cake-walk, because the prize to be won was a cake. This, in fact, formed the very centrepiece around which the couples moved in their 'march' or 'dance'. They vied with each other to excel in the way they walked, the intricacies of their fancy steps and their gracefulness, as well as, at times, the smartness of their dress. Those judged to have been the best performers 'took the cake'.

THIRD DEGREE

To be given the 'third degree' pictures a situation of the most severe interrogation, when a suspect is being grilled to tell the truth.

The phrase is now linked with criminal investigation in which the accused or the witness is cross-examined—without respite and with harshness—to supply information he is thought to be holding back.

Some authorities believe that the 'third degree' started in

American legal practice, in which the crime of murder was graded. 'Murder in the first degree' was premeditated, while 'murder in the second degree' was judged to have been committed unintentionally. This led people—wrongly—to assume that there also existed murder of 'the third degree'.

This is mere fiction. There never was a 'third degree'. In any case, the derivation would make no sense, as in such a scale of degrees, the third one would have been the least severe.

In reality, the giving of the third degree goes back to Freemasonry. In its craft, this was the highest degree, that of the Master Mason. To advance to it, the candidate had to pass the most rigorous 'trial' of proficiency. As the workings of the Masonic craft—its 'rituals'—are kept secret from the general public, it did not take long for people to imagine that the test the mason had to pass to qualify for, and to be initiated into, the third degree, was the most punishing and frightening. And this is the real background of 'the third degree' and all it now means.

THREE MISFORTUNES IN A ROW

That bad news is received and misfortune experienced in a series of threes and mostly one following the other in quick succession is a widespread superstition. Many people are so convinced of its reality that having been struck twice, they anxiously and apprehensively wait for the third blow to fall.

The superstition is based on the gospel story which tells how Peter had denied knowing or in any way to have been associated with Jesus, and did so consecutively three times—'before the cock crowed'. The sequence of three calamitous messages or events is thus an echo, if not result of, Peter's threefold negation.

TICKER TAPE

People have always loved to show their admiration of heroes and celebrities on the occasion of their visit or homecoming. The way they did so has differed from country to country and through the ages.

A universal custom was to shower them with flowers. Americans, generally innovative and pragmatic, created the ticker-tape parade as their unique type of reception.

Just as in the confetti showered on a bridal couple, the paper substituted for the original (and much more costly) rice and grain, so the thin streamers of paper served as an economic, but most spectacular replacement of flowers.

Unforgettable, indeed, was the sight of tonnes of shredded paper cascading from up-high. To watch it being dropped out of the windows of skyscrapers onto the motorcade in which the person being honoured was driven along in an open car was an exciting experience. The procession, traditionally, went up Broadway, leading through the financial district to the city hall where the official reception took place. The choice of route almost preselected the throwing of ticker tape.

Originally, the quotations of the stock market used to be relayed by messengers, a wearisome and prolonged procedure. The introduction of the first stock ticker (in 1868) revolutionised the practice. Henceforth the latest figures on the market were made available almost instantly and received simultaneously by the thousands of clients and speculators. In 1902, the ticker ribbon was superseded by the so much cheaper 'ticker tape'. Once having fulfilled its function, it was of no further use. Huge quantities of it were thrown away. After all, it was a period when people were not yet concerned with environmental pollution.

New Yorkers then discovered how even this surplus refuse was not without value, but of great ceremonial usefulness.

Ingeniously utilised, it could provide some extra splendour in expressing the citizens' welcome to outstanding personalities coming to New York.

Historic was the ticker-tape parade that in 1927 honoured Charles Lindbergh, perhaps the first of its kind, with 1800 tonnes of streamers enveloping the procession.

Possibly the largest ticker-tape reception ever to be given welcomed John Glenn, the astronaut, on 1 March 1962, after his return from his orbital flight. Well-nigh 3500 tonnes of paper were showered on him!

TICKLED PINK

Those greatly pleased are 'tickled pink'. The colourful portrayal might well reflect their physical expression of feeling highly gratified. They blush with pleasure.

TIERED WEDDING CAKE

The first tiered wedding cake was baked in London about 40 years after the great fire (in 1666) had devastated a large part of the metropolis. In fact, the cake indirectly owes its prominent design of several layers to Christopher Wren, the famous architect who rebuilt the city.

St Bride's Church was one of the many buildings destroyed by the conflagration. (Its name has no connection with any bride, but stands for and honours St Bridget.) Its reconstruction, one of Wren's finest achievements, was admired not least for its attractive spire. He completed it in 1701. Among ecclesiastical buildings, its height was surpassed only by that of the spires of St Paul and the Catholic Westminster Cathedral. In no time St Bride's was counted as one of London's most conspicuous sights.

It so happened that a pastry cook had his bakery near the church. Situated on Ludgate Hill, it was in close proximity to the Fleet Street Prison. In the fortuitous ways of life, these various factors combined to create the tiered wedding cake!

At the time, marriages were not permitted to be solemnised for convicts. A compassionate clergyman, nevertheless, clandestinely did so. And the baker, whose identity is lost, is said on each occasion generously to have provided a cake for the celebration. Inspired by St Bride's new steeple, he adopted its tiered shape. Thus, to this very day, unknowingly to all concerned, every tiered wedding cake continues to copy Wren's masterpiece and carries on a tradition started to add beauty to the illegally performed nuptials of convicts.

TILL THE COWS COME HOME

In most European countries cows are kept in sheds during the winter. With the coming of spring, they are turned out to graze in the fields. They relish the fresh young grass, particularly after having been fed on hay and straw through the many and long winter months. If left to their own devices, it takes a long, long time 'till the cows come home'. They go on gorging themselves till an overfull and therefore painful udder makes them return to be milked.

TIPPLER

Those habitually enjoying intoxicating drinks in small quantities, are referred to as 'tipplers'. This is an obsolete description of a tapster. The choice of name is based on an old tradition and habit of those serving drinks. Whenever tapping from the barrel, they would sample a little of the liquor.

Tipsy

Anyone slightly inebriated is most likely to lose their balance. And, *tip*ping over, they became known as 'tipsy'.

Toff

Students of noble birth, enrolled in Oxford or Cambridge University, conscious of their high standing in society, conspicuously displayed it in public by wearing a special kind of academic cap. This was distinguished by a golden tassel or tuft, the gold appropriate to the high fees they paid. So noticeable and outstanding was their special mark, the tuft eventually was identified with the wearer of the cap and became his nickname. However, in the transfer from the cap to the person, the tuft was corrupted in speech to 'toff'. The name did not remain confined to the undergraduates of the renowned institutions of learning. Eventually, it was applied to any member of the 'upper class', of titled rank.

A final transformation was then experienced by the tassel turned 'toff'. It became a favourite description of snooty people who, without reason or merit, regarded themselves as superior and displayed their imagined status by showiness of dress and affectation in manner.

Closely related to the toff—linguistically at least—is the toupee, the French 'forelock' (*toupet*), now applied to a hairpiece worn by bald men; and German women's *Zopf*, their plaited 'pigtail'.

TOILET

Of the many euphemisms used for the smallest room in the house, toilet has proved one of the most lasting and widely accepted ones. French in origin, *toilette* is the diminutive for a cloth, *toile*, and therefore denoted a 'small cloth'.

To start with, in the seventeenth century, toilet described the act of putting on one's clothes. Within less than a century, its application was expanded to a 'toilet call'. This did not mean, as might be imagined, a visit to the bathroom or lavatory. It referred to a then common practice of ladies of society to receive early callers, while still in the process of getting dressed. Toilet now implied a dressing-room.

Americans were the first to use toilet in the sense of the English water closet, the WC.

It is an odd fact that the French, always so logical and elegant, found no reason to camouflage the function of this so necessary convenience, if provided for men. They called a public urinal just what it was—a *pissoir*.

TOILET PAPER

Though the most widespread daily applied utility, little thought is given to the origin of toilet paper nor to its inventor, Joseph C. Gayetty of New York. Proud of his product, he had his name watermarked on each sheet. He first marketed it in 1857. Advertising it—very personalised—as 'Gayetty's Medicated Paper', he recommended it as 'a pure article for the toilet and a prevention for piles'! It is said that the early specimens were made of pearl-coloured manila hemp paper. The product was sold in bundles of 500 sheets, at 50 cents per packet. Its present-day description as toilet paper goes back only to the 1880s.

Tom cat

Male cats are toms. Generally it is believed that this name, a common abbreviation of Thomas, was given them for the sole reason of identifying their sex. But this is not the true ancestry of its designation.

'Ram' used to be the customary description of a male feline. That the ram was replaced by the tom is due to a story published anonymously in 1760. Entitled *The Life and Adventures of a Cat*, it caught people's imagination and gained nationwide popularity. It so happened that its male character was 'Tom the Cat'. The association became a permanent one.

Tongue in cheek

To say anything with the tongue in one's cheek is almost a physical impossibility. Thus positioned, the tongue would be immobilised or so restricted in its movement that any words would become indistinct and garbled beyond recognition. In fact, no one nowadays takes the words literally. The phrase is seen as a mere figure of speech. Those who speak with their 'tongue in cheek' really do not mean what they say. Their remarks are insincere or derisive.

And yet, what is now a mere metaphor, not to be taken literally, once was done. The practice of talking with one's tongue in the cheek is an early example of body language. Just as today people wink at a person to let them know that whatever they said was not intended to be taken seriously, and that they are only 'kidding', so, formerly, they conveyed this message by another type of body language. They pushed their tongue into one of their cheeks, causing it conspicuously to bulge. Their gesture could not be missed or mistaken.

Eventually, the practice was abandoned. But memories of it survived and its description became an idiom of everyday speech.

It is assumed that the gesture was rarely if ever used. Much more likely, hence, is the suggestion that the popular expression was merely the imaginative invention of an English clergyman. The Reverend Richard Barham was renowned for his humour. A minor canon at St Paul's, he became famous as an author and, in fact, the metaphor has been traced to him and his story of 'The Black Mousquetaire' which, in 1840, he included in his collection of The Ingoldsby Legends. It appears there in connection with a Frenchman's (ironic) remark about something being superb and magnificent. After quoting the words, Barham adds in brackets that they were spoken 'with his tongue in his cheek'. Other writers adopted his phrase which thus became part of the English language.

TOSSING A COIN

In the beginning, tossing a coin to decide an issue was rooted in the superstitious belief that the way the coin fell was not accidental, but directed by a superior power. It was the divinity that caused 'heads' or 'tails' to come up.

An ancient method of divination, it revealed the gods' message of which way to go and what to do. More than that, it indicated their wish, which was synonymous with a command. No one would dare to ignore it.

History played an additional part in the adoption of the practice and even was responsible for the terminology, possibly going back to Julius Caesar's time. His head was embossed on one side of every coin. To settle an argument, people tossed a coin. The person for whom Caesar's head showed up was right. The decision was not arbitrary, but like a royal command. No one would dispute it.

Superstition, divination and early authoritarianism thus combined to create the now so innocuous practice of tossing a coin.

TRIVIA

There is a trivial explanation for all trivia. From the Latin, it refers to the intersection of 'three roads'—tri via.

Such a location was very public and, in the early days of leisurely traffic, the crossroads served as a meeting place for all kinds of people. Coming from three directions and possibly from far away, they were only too ready to stop for a while, to exchange gossip, tittle-tattle of little consequence. Their interchange of news and views was soon identified with the very site where it occurred as 'three-ways'—trivia!

Going to the other extreme, trivia have been derived not from a mere junction of streets and things happening there, but from academic life. In medieval times, studies of the liberal arts were divided into seven subjects. These were taken up according to a fixed schedule and sequence. Students who, for instance, enrolled at Cambridge University did so at the age of 14, if not before, when their only knowledge was a smattering of elementary Latin. After a preliminary introduction into Latin grammar, they took up a course in logic. This was followed by the study of rhetoric based on the Latin text of Aristotle's treatise on the subject.

On having finished this part of their studies, the students became 'commencing bachelors'. Thus promoted, they advanced to the second and much more profound part of their training. A four-year course, it was comprised of four subjects: arithmetic, geometry, music and astronomy. Its successful conclusion qualified them as masters of arts which entitled them to become lecturers themselves.

Because of the number of subjects studied during this second part of the curriculum, this became known as the 'fourfold' course, in Latin the *quadrivium*. In distinction and appropriately, the much less onerous and exacting preceding three-year study of three comparatively minor and basic topics was designated the 'threefold' course or, once again using the Latin tongue, the *trivium*. Thus, the present-day 'trivia' (its plural), however trivial, mundane and unacademic, may well be the product of Cambridge University!

TRUTH IS STRANGER THAN FICTION

The proverbial expression that 'truth is stranger than fiction' is a condensation of Lord Byron's observation in *Don Juan*, which he wrote in 1823 (canto XIV: st. 101): 'Tis strange—but true; for truth is always strange,—Stranger than fiction.'

TURN THE TABLES

In a reversal of fortune it can be said that the tables are turned.

The phrase has been traced to board games, such as draughts, chess and backgammon in which, suddenly, the winning player becomes the loser. It has even been suggested that, far from being a mere figure of speech, the saying recalled a ruse. The change of luck was the result of opponents about to be beaten, by surreptitiously reversing the board ('turning the table') placing themselves on the winning side.

A second derivation links the saying with entertaining guests, and a very practical type of table once in existence. It fulfilled a dual purpose: for meals to be served on and as a workbench. For this reason its top was reversible. The side with a smooth surface was used for eating, and the other side, the rough one, used for manual chores. To turn the table on a visitor for the rough side to be on top, without saying a single word, clearly indicated how busy one was. Work had to be done and there was no time to act as a host to serve food. The message could not be missed.

Totally different and far-fetched, both in time and credibility, is the claim that the phrase goes back to ancient Roman days and an argument between spouses. It concerned money spent, or rather wasted. In those days, it is said, men liked to own tables of the most expensive timber and therefore highly priced. They had no qualms about purchasing them. When chiding their wives for having been too extravagant in spending money on unnecessary luxuries for their own pleasure, literally as it were, these turned the tables on them—as a silent reminder of their own wastefulness. Their gesture was well understood and fulfilled the purpose.

TURNCOAT

Turncoats who, without qualms of conscience, change their allegiance to the opposite side, take their name from mercenaries of former days. These military merchants, as they could be called, sold their martial services. They fought in wars not because they were conscripted or believed in the cause. Though adventurers, their main motive was the money they were paid for their services.

In those days uniforms were not camouflaged. On the contrary, they were distinctly and conspicuously coloured. The purpose of the practice, of course, was clearly to identify the country or the army for which the soldier was fighting and therefore to be able to distinguish between friend and foe. It also added to men's morale and their sense of pride.

When a mercenary realised that the forces he had joined were about to lose the battle, his only concern was to save his own life. With this aim in mind, he took off his uniform jacket and turned it inside out. All that was now visible was the coat's lining. Of a drab and unidentifiable colour, it would hide his former allegiance. He was truly a turncoat.

TWO STRINGS TO A BOW

For millennia, one of the chief weapons employed in warfare was the bow and arrow. They proved their value equally in hunting. During the pursuit of an enemy or a quarry, it sometimes happened that the string broke, rendering the weapon useless. Wisely, therefore, warriors and hunters carried with them (at least) a second string to their bow. In case of emergency, it was of inestimable worth, possibly preventing the loss of (one's) life or prey.

Though the bow and arrow are obsolete now, except in sport, they have left their impact on speech. In pursuit of an aim, it is always wise to have in reserve an alternate plan, in case the first one fails. Those adhering to this principle can well be described as having 'two strings to their bow'.

UNCLE SAM

'Uncle Sam' became the nickname for the Americans during the 'War of 1812' between Britain and the United States.

At the time, Samuel Wilson, a meat packer and former bricklayer, worked for his uncle, Elbert Anderson, who had a store yard at Troy on the Hudson River in the state of New York. His firm had the contract to supply meat (mostly beef and salted pork) to the army. They despatched it in large barrels.

Samuel Wilson was given the task of inspecting on behalf of the government each delivery. If passing it as fit for consumption, he stamped the individual container with a sign, indicating his approval. The mark chosen was four capital letters: EAUS. They represented the initials of Elbert Anderson's name and those of the United States.

One day, so a story goes, a visitor to the packing shed was intrigued by the four characters on the consignments and asked what they meant. Pulling his leg, one of the workers explained to him that they stood for Elbert Anderson's 'Uncle Sam'. The choice of 'Uncle Sam' in this instance was very appropriate. It was the nickname given to Samuel Wilson both inside and outside the firm. He was a well-known and liked identity in the city. What was meant as a joke was taken seriously and soon adopted far and wide, as the personification of the American. The authorities welcomed this as, at the time, they realised the role 'Uncle Sam' could play as a forceful symbol and propaganda weapon against mighty John Bull, representing the hostile British.

When, in 1854, at the ripe old age of 88, Samuel Wilson passed away, his name did not die with him and as 'Uncle Sam' it has been adopted worldwide as a nickname for a typical American and then for the entire American nation.

Years later, in 1868, a cartoonist's art created the picture of the Uncle Sam as it is known today. He was Thomas Nast, who worked for *Harper's Weekly*. Oddly, he transferred to him features, such as the goatee beard and the stars on the vest, he had previously used in the drawing of a famous clown.

UNDER THE WEATHER

Who would imagine that those who complain to be 'under the weather' are all at sea. The phrase—a cliché now—which describes a feeling of being unwell, often accompanied by a mood of dejection, was born on the ocean.

During a gale, seafarers used to take shelter below the deck. In every sense of the phrase, they placed themselves '*under* the weather'. As it were, they went the opposite way to those being on 'cloud nine'.

UPPER CRUST

Speaking of the 'upper crust' makes one immediately think of people at the top, constituting what was once called the 'upper class'. Actually, to start with, the expression was used very literally. It goes back to medieval banquets, when dinner plates were still unknown. Round loaves then took their place. Cut in half, each part served as a plate. Once the guest had consumed the food heaped on their bread 'plates', they finished up the meal by eating them as well. There were no leftovers and no need to wash up.

As the upper crust of the loaf was by far the better one, it was reserved for the most honoured and important guests. Though a long-forgotten custom, it is recalled in daily conversation, without the crust having become stale. It is used whenever people refer to those making up the elite of society as the 'upper crust'.

UPSHOT

The ultimate result of something undertaken is known as its 'upshot'. A sporting term, the final (and parting) shot in an archery match was once so called. Most likely, it received its name because the shot was aimed upward, into the air.

URCHIN

To refer to a mischievous and scruffy youngster as an urchin bestows on them (slightly streamlined to the modern tongue) the archaic name of a hedgehog. Several reasons have contributed to the peculiar choice.

Hedgehogs often proved a nuisance. Their continuous poking around in search of food did all kinds of damage. Though they consume a lot of harmful insects, they also have a taste for eggs, in pursuit of which they raid many nests. And was not a street urchin equally destructive to their environment? Like the hedgehog, they, too, are a source of irritation, rough and prickly just like this spiky creature.

Going back much further in time and to the world of the occult, it was also once believed that an evil spirit or mischievous goblin possessed the animal—at least for some periods of time, The peculiar noise of its snorting made people imagine that the uncanny sound revealed their presence. No wonder, therefore, that troublesome young people were likened to the hedgehog. Its early name of urchin has long been discarded, but the superstition associated with it concerning the devilish ghosts that inhabited it has survived in the modern street urchin. It has been seen as an explanation for their ragged appearance and unsavoury demeanour.

VENT ONE'S SPLEEN

Vent one's spleen

One of the misconceptions of early medicine concerned the spleen. It was regarded as the seat of morose feelings and irascibility. Tantrums of people were diagnosed as the result of a malfunction of their spleen. A substance it secreted made them so ill-tempered. Therefore, it was said of them that they released or 'vented' their spleen.

WALLOP

WALLS HAVE EARS

WARDROBE

WARM THE COCKLES OF ONE'S HEART

WASHOUT

WEAR ONE'S HEART ON ONE'S SLEEVE

WET BEHIND THE EARS

WET BLANKET

WHALE OF A TIME

WHIPPING BOY

WHISTLE FOR IT

WHITE FLAG

WILD GOOSE CHASE

WIMP

WIND UP A COMPANY

WINDFALL

WORCESTERSHIRE SAUCE

WALLOP

How a wallop became synonymous with a blow or spanking has been explained both in fact and in fiction.

The term has been traced to the Old Norman French *waloper*, meaning 'to gallop'. A rider who proved superior to another horseman had 'walloped' them! Also, those harshly knocked about might feel like being struck by the hoofs of a galloping horse. From its equine source, the wallop spread to any life situation that implied some kind of beating.

Wallop has been linked as well with a naval encounter said to have taken place in 1514. At the time, the French fleet made frequent raids on parts of the southern coast of Britain. On one occasion, they even succeeded in destroying by fire the city of Brighton, then still known as Brighthelmstone. To stop such incursions, King Henry VIII called on Admiral Sir John Wallop, one of his most outstanding naval commanders. He was instructed not only to repel any further attacks, but by retaliatory action make the marauders pay dearly for what they had done.

Wallop duly executed the task. He inflicted severe damage on the French, destroying numerous villages and ports on their coastline. Indeed, he thrashed the enemy so thoroughly that, in admiration, the British came to identify his name with any battering or pounding inflicted on an opponent. In this meaning to 'wallop' entered the dictionary as a strange (and unreal) war memorial, honouring the memory of an admiral who knew how to give a beating to those who well deserved it.

WALLS HAVE EARS

'Walls have hears' is a centuries-old warning. It calls on people to take caution in what they say, even in the privacy of their homes. 'Careless talk costs lives' was a widely displayed slogan during the Second World War.

Modern life has given the admonition increased validity. Bugging rooms and buildings has become a common practice, almost a routine operation of any secret service or devious commercial interests.

The saying originally was no mere figure of speech. To start with, more than 2000 years ago, it was taken very literally and it could truly be stated that walls had ears.

No doubt Dionysius, the 'tyrant of Syracuse', in Sicily, who ruled in the fifth century BC, was an early forerunner of twentieth-century demagogues. He anticipated their cruel treatment of political opponents and prisoners of war. At his command, captured Athenian soldiers were incarcerated in a quarry at Syracuse. There they were forced to live in filth and starved of food. Ingeniously, he had an artificial ear, said to be shaped like a real one, built into the walls of the prison. It enabled the guards to overhear whatever was discussed by the men inside.

The saying that walls have ears therefore was not coined by an imaginative mind, but based on an historic fact.

Catherine de Medici (1519–89), King Henry II's wife, was known for her selfishness and as a stirrer. Cleverly, she updated and expanded the use of the ancient tyrant's device. She copied the idea in her palace, the famous Louvre. She had hidden tubes inserted in the walls of the various rooms, all of them leading into her chamber. Thus she could hear whatever was being said 'within four walls'. It gave her due forewarning of plots against her life and information that proved invaluable in her scheming.

WARDROBE

The wardrobe now is a closet or cupboard provided to hang up one's clothes. As in the case of so many items of fashion, this term as well is an import from France. Warder robe, in the French tongue, was 'to guard the robe'—the real function of the modern piece of furniture.

Historically, this wardrobe can be traced back to a steward specially employed in the homes of nobility and royalty. It was his responsibility to take care and keep an eye on the precious ceremonial dresses, the robes of state. Accordingly, he was known as the warder of the robes—the first human wardrobe.

Eventually, his name was transferred to the part of the house or castle which was his domain and in which he guarded the garments. Life became more simple, dresses less numerous and the room or rooms once needed to store the many robes were reduced to a plain piece of furniture, as it were a mini-version of the original cloakroom, the present-day wardrobe.

WARM THE COCKLES OF ONE'S HEART

To 'warm the cockles of one's heart' portrays genuine delight and gratification. Paradoxically, the figure of speech is based on an ancient fallacy and an outdated medical description.

Excitement causes the heart to beat faster. Its noticeable palpitation, as is known now, is the result of additional adrenaline entering the bloodstream. Early on, however, the strange sensation led to the misconception that the heart actually controlled and ruled emotion, thereby confusing a mere symptom with the cause.

When seventeenth-century anatomists dissected the heart, the shape and surface of its ventricles reminded them of cockle shells. That is how their impression entered the loom of language and—metaphorically speaking—attached the shellfish to the human heart. Though not identified with it, it still serves it in the popular idiom giving voice to one's strong feelings of pleasure and satisfaction.

WASHOUT

For a complete failure or disappointment to be known as a 'washout' can have several reasons. It may recall a debacle, of minor or major degree. Heavy rains which caused a picnic to be called off literally washed it out. Roads and railway lines become impassable by having been 'washed out' by a flash flood or inundation. In the navy, 'washout' was the slang for the cancellation of an order and very understandably so. The order used to be recorded in chalk on a slate. If the signal was voided or had been transmitted, it was duly 'washed out'.

Militarily, a washout used to designate the end of a shooting practice. The choice of word here, too, was justified and based on a procedure followed. To prepare the target for the next squad, all traces left from the previous exercise were obliterated. The bull's eye was blackened and bullet holes were covered up with white paint—literally they were whitewashed. The routine possibly was responsible for not only the 'washout' but the 'whitewash' as well.

Water fulfilled a useful function in the mining of gold. It helped separate the ore from the dirt, by washing away the latter. For this purpose boxes were placed at strategic points. But everything comes to an end, and so did the supply of alluvial gold. When miners discovered that the containers were washed clean, they voiced their disappointment by saying that they were 'washed out'. Their description of this fact lent itself fittingly to any other situation that had come to a sad ending, proving a failure one way or another.

WEAR ONE'S HEART ON ONE'S SLEEVE

Whoever wears their heart on their sleeve openly displays their innermost feelings.

The now puzzling expression can be traced to the medieval days of chivalry. Knights fighting in a tournament wanted everyone to know for whom they fought. Proudly and conspicuously they thus wore something the lady of their choice had given them as a token of her affection. It could be a ribbon, a scarf, or a handkerchief. Records of the time tell that 'Maydes and gentlewomen gave to their favourites, as tokens of their love, little handkerchiefs of about three or four inches square, wrought round with a button at each corner'. (The button, it has been suggested, in fact was a tassel.)

The knight tied (or pinned) the treasured gift to his sleeve. Therefore it was true to say that, contrary to hiding his attachment, he wore his heart (or rather his heart's desire) on his sleeve.

The days of chivalry have long gone. But the knights' practice of broadcasting their attachment to a lady in so special a way is recalled in what is now merely a phrase. Not least, we still use it because Shakespeare immortalised it in *Othello* where Iago professes to Roderigo a devotion which he really did not have:

> For when my outward action doth demonstrate
> The native act and figure of my heart
> In compliment extern, 'tis not long after
> But I will wear my heart upon my sleeve
> For daws to peck at: I am not what I am.

WET BEHIND THE EARS

To refer to those immature and gullible as still 'wet behind the ears' is due to an early observation made in stables and in cowsheds. Having watched calves and foals being born and then licked dry by their mother, it was noticed that the last place to be 'dried' was behind the ears.

WET BLANKET

A wet blanket comes in handy to put out flames and thereby to avoid a dangerous conflagration. Its dampening effect made people use it as a metaphor for killjoys who delight in spoiling people's fun and in discouraging their adventurous spirit by giving all kinds of reasons against what they are about to do. Like a wet blanket, they put out the fire of enthusiasm and dampen all joy and pleasure.

WHALE OF A TIME

Those who have a 'whale of a time' certainly are enjoying themselves. The metaphor pictures the extent of their excessive pleasure by comparing it to the enormous size of the whale. The largest animal alive, a blue whale may grow to a length of 30 metres (100 feet) and weigh up to 150 tonnes.

WHIPPING BOY

To make others take one's place, particularly for an unpleasant task, has been an age-old practice. In early religion, man thus used to substitute animals for himself as a sacrificial offering to the gods! It is the origin of the scapegoat.

At one time, in parts of Europe, youths conscripted into the army were permitted to hire a 'replacement' to fight and, if fate so willed it, to be killed in their stead.

Royalty provided their own type of surrogate. It took the form of the whipping boy. Now merely used as a striking metaphor, originally it was a very realistic designation.

Children will be children, even if they are young princes. Their behaviour, too, at times merited punishment. However, being of royal blood, it was regarded below their status for them to be chastised in the way of common folk by corporal punishment.

Whenever the necessity arose to teach the prince a lesson, his punishment was transferred to a boy specially kept at court for that purpose, and aptly called the 'whipping boy'. The institution of this royal scapegoat no longer exists. Nevertheless, its memory survives in the figure of speech, now applied to many new situations.

WHISTLE FOR IT

Anyone told that they can 'whistle for it' is left in no doubt that they can just as well forget all about what they expect to obtain. Oddly, the words, which could be regarded as almost rude, have a ritual background, with exactly the opposite meaning. They go back to the belief once held that in a becalmed sea, whistling by sympathetic magic could raise the much-needed wind.

Interpreted differently, the rejection might equally imply that whoever is asking for something, has no chance of getting it. The best thing for them to do is, in the tradition of outdated superstition, whistle for it. It will have the same (non) effect.

WHITE FLAG

Military units used to march into battle conspicuously displaying their colours. It challenged the enemy and inspired the company. A white flag—on the other hand—represents the opposite. Lacking identifying marks, it was ineffective, both as a demonstration of defiance and a motivating force. Therefore, showing a white flag indicates a plea for truce or readiness to surrender.

WILD GOOSE CHASE

People who pursue a hopeless and almost unattainable task are said to go on a 'wild goose chase'. Oddly, the metaphor originated in horseracing.

A popular game in Elizabethan times was a race between equestrians. Anyone could take the lead. But once he had succeeded in doing so, all the others had to follow him, at regular intervals. However, his route was not predetermined. The successful rider could go off in any direction he fancied, which made it very difficult, if not impossible, for the others to keep up with him. The fact that the rest of the field had to follow the leader whichever way he went reminded people of the flight of wild geese, which likewise followed the leading bird, not knowing where.

Shakespeare, as with so many other idioms, popularised the comparison. In *Romeo and Juliet*, Mercutio expresses his inability to understand and keep up with Romeo's mind, saying, 'Nay, if thy wits run the wild goose chase, I have done'.

Times changed and, with them, people's pursuits. The horsey 'wild goose chase' went out of fashion and all that was remembered of it was the erratic course it once took.

People have short memories and when Dr Johnson came to define the phrase, unaware of its real beginning and context, he saw in it 'a pursuit of something as unlikely to be caught as a wild goose'. His explanation made sense and the lexicographer's authority assured that his interpretation has been retained ever since.

WIMP

A vogue word of the late twentieth century is the wimp. This description may well have shrunk from a 'whimper' when asked to take decisive action and show strength of character. A jellyback in his or her lack of courage, a wimp is one who makes a whining, plaintive response, signifying and achieving nothing.

WIND UP A COMPANY

When a company is liquidated and its assets distributed, it is said to be 'wound up'. Would it not be so much more appropriate to speak of its being 'wound down'? After all, when a clock is wound up, it works. Wound down, it stops.

The term might have originated in early mining. When all the coal had been brought to the surface and the mine, exhausted, was about to be closed, the last bucket was hauled to the top. It was 'wound up' by means of a rope around a windlass—and that was the end of the mine.

On the other hand, the apparently paradoxical use of the phrase may come from hand spinning and the practice of taking the 'loose ends' from a fleece of wool to 'wind (them) up' into a tidy ball. Winding up of a company frequently implies the unravelling of the tangled mess in which it has ended up. The similarity of situation equally could have been responsible for referring to the closure of a firm as being 'wound up' and not wound down, just like those loose ends of woollen thread.

In a similar vein, a speaker winds up a talk or a chairperson a discussion. Either of them does so by gathering in—summing up—the various strands of thought or points of view expressed and, with it, concludes the discussion or discourse.

WINDFALL

A good fortune unexpectedly coming one's way is referred to as a 'windfall'. Originally, the term really meant what it said. It had its beginning in Britain and goes back to British members of nobility, whose estate often included large tracts of forest. In spite of their owning them, they were not permitted to make free use of their trees. Much less so, of course, could any commoner.

To protect forests is not a modern phenomenon. Long before the ecological concern shown by conservationists and environmentalists, royalty pursued and enforced an identical policy. However, they did so with a totally different aim in mind. They were prompted by considerations of national defence.

At the time, Britain's rule and defence greatly depended on its fleet. To maintain a sufficient number of ships was paramount. For this reason, it was decreed that no tree could be felled or timber cut except for the purpose of building vessels for the Royal Navy.

There was one exception. Trees uprooted by storms or branches blown down by a strong wind were free for the taking. In every sense of the word, they became a 'windfall'.

WORCESTERSHIRE SAUCE

Worcestershire sauce, now used in many parts of the western world, recalls the English county where it was first produced.

While serving as the Governor of Bengal, this province of former British India, in the early 1880s, Lord Sandys had taken a special liking to one of its many spicy sauces. This prompted him, at the end of his term of office, to obtain its recipe before returning to England. Soon after settling down again in his home town of Worcester, he took the 'formula' to the local pharmacy. He asked John Wheeley Lea and William Perrin, its joint owners, whether they could make up the 'prescription' for him. They agreed at once. Astute businessmen, they welcomed it as an opportunity to expand their enterprise with a new sideline. For this reason they far exceeded the quantity Lord Sandys had ordered. The surplus they kept for themselves, with the intention in the not too distant future of marketing it as a new product.

However, when, with great expectation, they tasted the novel sauce, they were horrified. Of a sharp and pungent flavour, it was most unsuitable for the English palate. After all, it would not pay them to take up this new line! Nevertheless, they did not pour away the mixture. They bottled it and stored it in the basement.

They had forgotten all about it until one day, by mere chance, they came across the jars. Something prompted them to check their contents. Having matured meanwhile, the liquid had acquired a piquant flavour, quite unusual and now most pleasing and so different from what it had been before.

Immediately they realised that, after all, there was a commercial potential in the sauce. It was a real treasure. They alone in Britain had the recipe and thus only they knew how to mix it and, not least, to let it mature. They now seriously embarked on making it, calling their novel dark brown concoction Lea and Perrin's Worcestershire Sauce. It gave the

English county, already famous for its porcelain and bone china, yet another reason to become world-renowned. The label on the bottle proudly stated that the sauce was 'the original and genuine [product] from the recipe of a nobleman in the county'. It did not reveal who he was.

YANK
YEN
YUPPIE

YANK

That Americans are known as Yanks is only for foreign consumption. In the United States, Yank is applied merely to someone from the north, mainly from New England, and in many cases then in not too complimentary a way. It is a legacy of the Civil War (1861–65), when the soldiers of the Confederate Army of the South used the term disparagingly for the members of the (northern) federal troops, the Union Army. A multitude of explanations has been given for the name. Most of these are conjectures or the product of uninformed imagination.

Thus it has been (wrongly) claimed that the Yank was the result of American Indians' difficulty in properly pronouncing the name of the 'English' occupying their territory. On their tongue, it sounded very much like Yangeeze. Soon changed into Yankee, finally it was shortened to Yank.

Equally without foundation is the assertion that the name was the mispronounced American Indians' word for 'silent'. Themselves comparatively taciturn, they were struck by white men's almost constant talk. Cynically, they had dubbed them the 'silent' people.

More fallacious still, apart from being unkind, is a suggestion which traced the word to the Cherokee dialect in which *eankee* was said to be used for a 'coward'.

Most likely, Yank came from Janke, the Dutch diminutive for Jan, the English Johnny. Its adoption for Americans was due to a chain of events now part of history. It goes back, first of all, to the days of Dutch colonisation which preceded colonisation by the English, when New York was still known as New Amsterdam.

Already in Europe a Dutchman (or Hollander), because of his love of cheese, mockingly had been nicknamed by others, Jan Kaas—which would be Johnny Cheese in English. Telescoped into Jankaas, eventually it produced 'Yankee'. He carried with him to America his peculiar description with its cheesy association.

Soon, however, the Dutch connection was forgotten and the nickname assumed a contemptuous meaning. Reversing the sides, the Hollanders now described some of the English settlers, particularly those who had moved to New England, by their own former epithet, not least because of the New Englanders' (lack of) business ethics. To the Dutchmen's strict standards, these seemed to leave much to be desired. But their attempt misfired. The English took the implied criticism of what they regarded as their commercial astuteness as a compliment and, proudly, began to call themselves Yanks!

As time passed, all the New Englanders were so named. Still, even this was not the end of it. At the outbreak of the Revolutionary War, the English dubbed all Americans by the name. During the Civil War this was then once again restricted to the north.

A description introduced to humiliate and deride cheese lovers, in a circuitous route, had been changed into a name of pride and honour, respect and disrespect, always depending on the circumstances and by whom it was used. The fate of the 'Yank', indeed, reflects the vagaries of history and vicissitudes of a simple nickname.

YEN

Anyone who has an intense craving for something is said to have a 'yen' for it. As so many people desire wealth above all things, it is understandable that it has wrongly been assumed that the yen referred to the well-known Japanese monetary unit. Its name is derived from the Chinese *yüan*, depicting a circular object, shaped as round as a coin.

However, the type of (emotional) yen possessing people, though also Chinese in its source, comes from the Cantonese, in which language the original *yan* is (nothing but) 'smoke'. Significantly, the smoke in this case is that from an opium pipe, desperately clamoured for by addicts.

It could also be that far from being Oriental in origin or belonging to the drug culture, the yen is merely a simplified and greatly contracted version of *yearn*(ing).

YUPPIE

The popularity of acronyms made people soon forget what they represented. A combination of initials in reality, they were (mis)taken for proper words. Their number now is so great that special dictionaries list and explain them.

The 1980s created the 'yuppie'. They are members of the ambitious and affluent but reckless young generation. They love the good life and anything money can buy. They wear fashionable designer clothes, sport expensive watches and fill well-paid jobs in their professions. They drive fast and flashy cars and live in showy homes, located in suburbs renowned for wealth.

So distinguished, they were given their own label. A member of this group was identified as a '*y*oung *u*rban *p*rofessional', popularly shortened to yuppie. In people's minds, the nickname reflected their conspicuous lifestyle and ostentatious place in society.

ZILCH

ZILCH

Zilch is 'nothing'. As a cartoon character which appeared in the 1930s in *Ballyhoo*, an American magazine, he was conspicuous by his absence. Nevertheless, everyone was very conscious of his presence. This was shown by the reaction of young girls who, almost completely naked, were portrayed in very suggestive poses. Looking askance at a pile of shed clothing or a leg sticking out from behind a sofa, they exclaimed, 'Oh, Mr Zilch!'.

With nothing really to be seen, Mr Zilch's identity was never established and assumed the present-day meaning. He was a man that was not there.

The figure of the cartoon duplicated the then typical caricature of a college boy who was a 'good for nothing'. Known as Joe Zilch, he was of identical (in)significance and (lack of) presence. Whatever he said was meaningless, mere gibberish.

Maybe totally divorced from any person, however great a nonentity, zilch might combine fractions of three nothings, expressed in different languages: the English zero, the Latin *nil* and the German *Nichts*. This may be so, even though three times zero, in whichever tongue, adds up to nothing!

INDEX